TEN MEN AND COLCHESTER

TEN MEN AND COLCHESTER

Public Good and Private Profit in a Victorian Town

by

ANDREW PHILLIPS

ESSEX RECORD OFFICE
CHELMSFORD
1985

First published 1985
by the Essex Record Office,
County Hall
Chelmsford
CM1 1LX

© Essex County Council

Essex Record Office Publication No. 89

ISBN 0 900360 65 8

Origination by A3 Typesetting Studio, Colchester. Printed
by Anchor Brendon Ltd., Tiptree.

CONTENTS

ILLUSTRATIONS

Acknowledgements: Thanks are extended to the following institutions and individuals for granting reproduction facilities and permission: Colchester & Essex Museum, nos. 3, 4, 9, 10, 14, 15, 16, 17, 18, 23, 25, 27, 28, 29, 30, 31, 34, 36, 37, 38, 40, 41, 45; Essex Library, Local Studies Dept., Colchester, nos. 2, 6, 8, 19, 20, 22, 32, 33, 42, 43; Anglian Water Authority, nos. 11, 35; Essex County Newspapers, no. 44, Suffolk Record Office, Ipswich Branch, no. 7; G. W. Martin, no. 21. The back cover and chapter endings are from 'The ABC Guide to the Colchester Municipal Elections' by Gurney Benham, published with the **Colchester Gazette,** 29th October, 1890.

PREFACE

'Do not judge a book by its cover' – should one judge it by its preface either? This book tells a story. It is written to entertain, but the narrative style also permits an analysis that might otherwise be lost. Studies of Victorian cities are frequently atomised: public health, urban politics, railway development, municipal socialism are studied thematically. The smaller Victorian town, however, experienced them as one, and Colchester was a smaller town, albeit the largest in Essex. Hence the action of ten men might be vital to its development. What sort of men? We have inherited from the Victorians a habit of interpreting their history in moralistic terms: slum landlords, enlightened reformers, ruthless capitalists, christian philanthropists. Maybe they were the same people.

To many I owe my thanks: to Professor William Ashworth who must answer for my interest in Victorian England, to the staff of the Local Studies Library at Colchester for their help over many years, to Vic Gray and Paul Coverley of the Essex Record Office, to Jim Lee, formerly Engineer to the Colchester Waterworks and Barry Oakley of the Anglian Water Authority, to Hervey Benham, the champion of Peter Bruff, to Bronwen Wolton, my efficient and long-suffering typist, to my wife who corrected countless errors in the text and suffers my frequent disappearance into the past, and to Dr. David Stephenson for his comments on the manuscript and for first introducing me to this remarkable tale.

In assessing monetary values in this book it is worth recalling that in Victorian Colchester a farm labourer was paid from 9 to 15 shillings a week, while the Borough Council's annual income in the 1850s was less than £4,000. Inflation was unknown.

Prologue

On September 27th 1883 Colchester's giant water-tower was formally opened. The guest of honour at the ceremony, Sir Robert Rawlinson, himself near the end of a long career promoting public health, and conscious that the project had generated a certain controversy in the town, hastened to reassure his audience that not only was the Balkan Tower a wise investment, but that it would surely stand one hundred years. It has.

Whether that Victorian audience believed him, we do not know, but there is reason to think that a good many now doubted the wisdom of the entire project, and dared not think about its appalling cost. Stepping cautiously over ground made muddy by the recent rain only a few knew how close that day had come to cancellation. Edging into line for the official photo, they might heartily hope that the Balkan Tower controversy was over. How wrong they were – except in this respect. To them and every citizen of Colchester the Balkan Tower did not exist. Quite simply it was JUMBO, and has been ever since. Today it still dominates the town's western horizon, but familiarity even perhaps affection, has now replaced the outcry that greeted its construction. Sir Robert Rawlinson and all those guests have shuffled into history. Ten Men at least should be remembered . . .

Dramatis Personæ

(in order of appearance)

Peter Schuyler Bruff (1812-1900). Conservative. East Anglia's most colourful and successful civil engineer from the heroic age of railway building, who during a remarkably long and varied career was responsible for planning and constructing several hundred miles of railway, sundry harbour and coastal improvements, five piers, four waterworks, divers gasworks, sewage works, draining schemes and the Ipswich tramway. He also played a major role in the development of Walton and Clacton as seaside resorts. These activities inevitably spawned certain legal complications. Photo p19.

William Warwick Hawkins (1816-1868). Conservative. The dominant personality in mid-Victorian Colchester, he inherited from his father a flourishing timber business at the Hythe, built up during the Napoleonic Wars. He married into an old Tory family, but earned the distinction of becoming the only 19th-century Colchester businessman to be M.P. for the town. His determined but unsuccessful bid to develop the Hythe as a major port led to the building of two railways and a close relationship with Peter Bruff. His latter years were dogged by illness. Photo 47.

Charles Henry Hawkins (1818-1898). Conservative. Younger brother and business partner of William Hawkins, for 35 years he was a key figure in the Colchester Conservative Party, and, as a consequence, the management of the town – two closely related activities. Shrewd, determined and able, he was often accused by his opponents of political intimidation. When finally deposed by the Liberals his response was philosophical: "I have played political bowls all my life, and therefore must expect rubs . . . As I am of no further service, I respectfully wish you good day". He was a generous patron of charities. Photo p71.

John Taylor (1807-1867). Conservative. For 35 years proprietor and editor of the *Essex Standard,* Colchester's most successful and, for some years, only Colchester-printed newspaper, he showed a rare willingness to jeopardise his circulation (or to increase it) by his trenchantly-held beliefs. A moderate Conservative, Taylor came into bitter conflict with the Hawkins brothers and most of the party leadership. His outspoken attacks on political exclusiveness and the private profit of public measures reached a memorable climax shortly before his death. His motto, claimed his obituary, was "Is it right?". Photo p62.

John Bawtree Harvey (1809-1890). Liberal. Newspaper proprietor and printer, he was Colchester's most outstanding 19th-century public servant. Holder of over 20 elected offices, some for more than 40 years, to his admirers he epitomised the best of reforming Liberalism and devout nonconformity. An able businessman and a gifted public speaker with a bookish taste for learning, his courtesy and tact drew universal expressions of respect. But did such restraint best serve the partisan interests of the Colchester Liberal Party? Photo p39.

James Noah Paxman (1832-1922). Liberal. Colchester's most success-ful 19th-century businessman, he rose from humble (and carefully obscured) origins to establish, virtually single-handed, the engineering firm that for almost 100 years was the town's largest employer. Civic responsibility seemed a natural acknowledgement of these achieve-ments and his formidable will and consummate skill at public relations were a major asset to the local Liberal Party – particularly when the "water question" came to the boil. Photo p123.

Frederick Blomfield Philbrick (1809-1892). Liberal. Solicitor extra-ordinary, his sharp and fastidious mind secured him a string of appointments as legal adviser to several public companies (notably two railways), during a career that spanned over 50 years. A considerable political activist and a specialist at public indignation, he was Town Clerk of Colchester from 1836-37 and 1880-84. The interval between these periods of office is considerable. Therein lies a tale. Photo p79.

Henry Jones (1826-1889). Conservative. Son of a Waterloo hero, he passed a turbulent youth. Radical politics and a spell in the coal trade preceded a swift transition from breaking the law to interpreting it. Articled to a solicitor he rose to become one of East Anglia's most pugnacious and successful advocates. His business interests included a brickyard, two housing estates, an hotel and a laundry. From 1877 to 1880 he was Town Clerk of Colchester. Then the Liberals removed him. He was not amused. Photo p64.

Wilson Marriage (1843-1932). Liberal. Offspring of a notable Quaker family and proprietor with his father of East Mills, Colchester, he was perhaps the most able of late Victorian leaders in the town. A successful businessman, a campaigner for public education, public health and the closure of public houses, he was the driving force behind the building of a new Town Hall. The sewage in the river particularly annoyed him, but his efforts to remove it met with rather less success. Photo p84.

James Wicks (1835-1905). Liberal. Colchester's most explosive and controversial public figure, he inherited from his father a prosperous wine and spirit business. This however was always secondary to his single-minded devotion to the Radical wing of the Liberal Party. For ten years he battled for political supremacy, only to tie his fortunes to Jumbo the Water-tower. Things were never quite the same again. Tragedy haunted his final years, but he would have appreciated the newspaper headline that greeted his death: 'The Dead Champion', it said. Photo p95.

A stands for each politician's ADDRESS ;
    Some show it more and some show it less,
Some put in head-lines of extra black letter,
Some seem to think that the less said the better.

1

The First Thousand Years

Colchester has had a public water supply for a very long time. Partly this is a consequence of geology.[1] For mainly strategic reasons the Romans built the town on a hill, which to the north and east slopes down to the River Colne. The top fifty feet or so of soil is well-drained glacial sand and gravel left by the last ice age, but the retreating glacier which scoured out the river valley also cut through the strata exposing the London clay below. The result of this has always been apparent. As John Norden the topographer put it in 1594, Colchester:

"...... standeth upon moste sweete springes, trickelinge from the towne on all sydes".[2]

These natural springs occur where rainwater, draining through the sand and gravel onto the impermeable clay, runs along the junction of the strata to escape down the side of the hill.

Since no Roman wells have been found within the walls of the town, it seems likely that the Romans used the springs, particularly the most prolific which lie to the north-west of the town. This would explain the discovery in Balkerne Lane of several pressurised Roman water mains made up of jointed wooden pipes held together by iron bands. These were doubtless fed by the two largest springs, one at the bottom of Balkerne Hill and one, 400 metres to the west, in what was later called Chiswell Meadow.[3] It is even possible that the Sheepen Spring, a further 600 metres round the contour was also used. When this was taken into public use in the 19th century, evidence of 'Roman baths' was found, though what this amounted to is now unclear. The same claim was more reliably made for the Balkerne Spring, when waterworks were first built at the foot of Balkerne Hill in 1808. A good deal of Roman material was found, including wooden structures, perfectly preserved in the saturated ground.[4]Further evidence of Roman baths may therefore await some future excavation. However, these wooden structures might equally have been the framework for pumps or water wheels used to bring water up the hill, for the pressurised mains appear to converge upon the Balkerne Gate, and probably some sort of water-tower stood inside the gate, where lies the highest point of the Roman town. Such elevation would provide sufficient pressure to carry water to the present Long Wyre Street where Roman pipes have also been found. The site of Jumbo may thus have been in use for an identical purpose seventeen hundred years before the present tower was built.

It is also clear that in the Middle Ages conduits carried water from the springs. The court rolls of the 14th century report several disputes involving watercourses in the vicinity of Balkerne Hill. For example in 1330 one Simon Smelt was charged with stopping up his watercourse and making a pit beside the Roman wall so deep that North Gate and its environment was flooded. Later a cistern was built to hold the Chiswell Spring water, and in 1536 Henry Webbe, a wool merchant, carried its water, apparently by pipes, to his house on North Hill. For this privilege, which he doubtless shared with others, he paid an

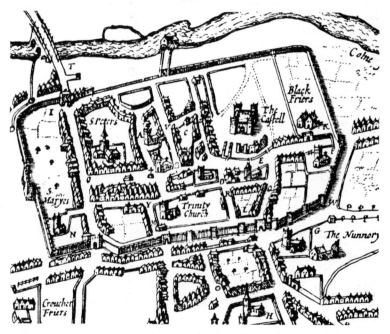

Speed's map of Colchester (1610) shows the walled town with, at the north-west, the water from Balkerne Spring skirting the wall, puncturing the building line and running in an open channel to the river at North Bridge. Middle Mill and the well in Stanwell Street are also marked, and in the south-east, at St. Botolph's Corner, the beginning of St. Botolph's Brook.

annual rent of fourpence. Spring water also served the brewery operated by Ralph Finch at the foot of Balkerne Hill, and in his will he provided for "the waters from the cistern" to:

"run in pipes of lead into the washing place at the Balkon, so that water should come into it clean, and not soyld with any kind of cattle or fowles . . ."

Channels marking this system are clearly shown on Speed's map of Colchester in 1610, running into the river above North Bridge.[5]

Shortly after this, something far more significant was attempted. Around 1620 a syndicate of businessmen or 'undertakers' built in Chiswell Meadow the Town Water House. From here they raised the water, probably by suction pumps, up the steep slope to a cistern or reservoir constructed on top, a site roughly equivalent to the western end of Papillon Road today. They were now at a sufficient elevation to pipe the water along the line of the present Papillon Road into the town.[6]

There was however a snag. The square of land the pipes crossed to reach the town, called Lord's Land, was then fields owned by Sir Thomas Lucas, Lord of the manor of Lexden. Growing friction between Colchester and the Lucas family in the years prior to the Civil War soon led to trouble for this, the town's first waterworks company. In 1633, following a complaint from his tenant, Sir Thomas cut the pipes in two. The undertakers, claiming that their water supply was both a vital security against fire and a great blessing to the poor, appealed for support to central government. Arbitration was attempted, but with Lucas demanding an annual rent of £3 and the undertakers offering 44 shillings, only government intervention settled the dispute. The water supply was restored, but not for long. Six years later Lucas again threatened action, this time because the undertakers, with commendable enterprise, were operating an ale house at the waterworks. The government now sided with Sir Thomas and summarily ordered the closure of the ale house. There matters rested until the Siege of Colchester in 1648, in which Sir Thomas's son, Sir Charles Lucas, played so prominent a part, this time from inside the town. Now it was the turn of the besieging Parliamentary army to tear up the pipes, partly to cut off the town's supply, partly to provide a welcome source of lead for making bullets. Doubtless they also destroyed, or at least incapacitated, whatever machinery the Town Water House boasted.[7]

The siege ground on to its melancholy end. Lucas was shot by firing squad, and though much in ruins, the town was heavily fined. In the miserable aftermath it is not surprising that the restoration of the waterworks was not a priority, and most of the citizens were now dependent on public wells within the walls. In fact it was 1685 before

John Wheeley, better remembered for his determined but unsuccessful attempts to demolish Colchester Castle, applied for and received permission to dig up the streets in order to restore a water supply based on the old Town Water House.[8] There were, however, disadvantages to this system, notably the distance from the town centre of the cistern beyond Lord's Land, and its lack of elevation. One of Wheeley's fellow contractors, John Potter, a cloth merchant and ex-mayor, therefore proposed alternative arrangements, which were introduced in 1707.

Potter reverted to the hill-top site just inside the Balkerne Gate once used by the Romans. In a field then owned by the parsonage of St Mary's-at-the-Walls, close to the Balkerne Gate, he constructed first one then two cisterns, each holding 15,000 gallons. Water was then raised from Chiswell Meadow, and carried by underground pipes through the arch of the Balkerne Gate into the cistern. From here it ran in pipes down Church Lane into the town. As part of the lease St Mary's parsonage received a free supply of water, reckoned to be worth £1 a year.[9] This compares exactly with the average annual water rate at Bath in the 18th century, and underlines the fact that at that time, a domestic supply of piped water was a comparative luxury.[10]

Indeed it is perhaps indicative of the early decline of the town's cloth trade that Potter's improved supply came to a halt in 1737, partly

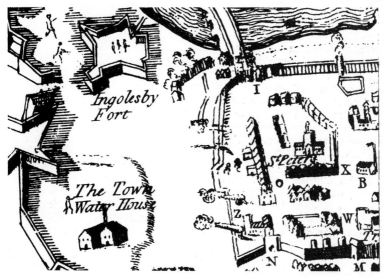

The Town Water House features in a plan showing the defences at the Seige of Colchester in 1648. If this drawing is accurate, can any technical deductions be made from the presence of a chimney?

because it was run inefficiently, but mainly because "the town growing poor was not well able to pay", an explanation provided by the then rector of St Mary's, the historian, Philip Morant, on whose parsonage field the cisterns stood. Morant therefore paid the late operators a small sum and dismantled the cisterns, reusing the bricks to repair one end of the rectory. Central Colchester was now without a piped supply, "to the inexpressible danger of the town in case a fire should happen", Morant lamented.[11]

The inhabitants meanwhile, as they had always done, made ample use of the river and a large number of both private and public wells, such as King Coel's Pump, substantially refurbished in 1763 on its earlier medieval site at the junction of High Street and Head Street.[12] Only at the bottom of North Hill was piped water from Chiswell Meadow still supplied. After travelling east along the contour, a chain of six cisterns, a reservoir and a pond distributed its water in equal divisions between three owners and six premises on both sides of North Hill. For an annual rental other households were allowed to draw from those cisterns to which there was public access.[13] One of them has given its name to Cistern Yard which is still marked near the bottom of North Hill. Such local arrangements could be found all over the town, based on wells and dipping places, which invariably marked an active spring.

King Coel's Pump in about 1770. Far left the inn sign of the Waggon and Horses at the top of North Hill; right foreground a waggon is loaded with Colchester bays for the London market. The ornamental gates behind, leading to St. Peter's church, were never built, the site being then occupied by the Dutch Bay Hall, and later by the Essex and Suffolk Fire Office.

This traditional picture was not disturbed until 1808 with the arrival in Colchester of Ralph Dodd, an adventurous civil engineer from London who proposed, but did not build, the first tunnel under the Thames, and died penniless with a string of distinguished failures to his name. In fine entrepreneurial style Dodd foisted himself upon the town, publishing impressive details of a proposed new Waterworks Company. He also took the trouble, which none of his predecessors had done, to have his proposals underwritten by an Act of Parliament, making sweeping promises to supply water to almost all corners of the borough – a fact that was to be of considerable importance later on. Water from Chiswell Meadow and the Balkerne Springs was gathered in first one and later two large reservoirs at the foot of Balkerne Hill, and a pumping house was built beside them to accommodate what was probably Colchester's first steam engine. 176 years later the same site is still used as a pumping station by the Anglian Water Authority. A large reservoir was also built inside the Balkerne Gate on the spot where Potter's cisterns had once stood, and Dodd's 'patent' water pipes were laid up Balkerne Hill from his new pumping station.[14]

Such impressive arrangements and a string of London backers did not however prevent a disastrous opening ceremony when

> "by the first stroke of the engine the pipes rent asunder like rotten paper, as had been predicted by everyone who saw them, and about 700 feet were rendered useless . . ."

Incompetence on this scale was particularly repellent to the man who dictated these remarks, the mayor, Thomas Hedge, a distinguished clock and watchmaker for whom precision engineering was a way of life. He was replying to an enquiry from Shropshire about the town's satisfaction with the new scheme. Writing in 1809 the mayor's amanuensis protested that Colchester still had no supply, while Dodd was busy replacing his 'patent' pipes with cast iron ones. Meanwhile shares in the new Company were changing hands in the London market with the frequency of a gambling operation.[15]

In all probability Dodd's pipes were not to blame. It seems more likely that he had failed to install adequate air chambers to his pumps, and suffered in consequence a water surge, the result of forcing a mobile substance like water uphill, when its natural inclination is to surge back with an equal and opposite force.[16]

These and other misadventures led Dodd to part company with his backers, and his last appearance in Colchester was in 1810 in a court of law, where he was found guilty of assault upon the Clerk of the Waterworks Company who had denied him access to the works.[17] Nevertheless – indeed, perhaps because of Dodd's departure – the new Waterworks survived, soon offering, as an additional service to the public, hot and cold baths, the former, heated by steam from the engine, costing two shillings a time.[18]

Almost contemporary with the establishment of the waterworks came another event significant for the future of the town. In the absence of action by the Corporation, there was re-established in 1811, also by Act of Parliament, the Channel and Paving Commissioners, a body of leading inhabitants with power to raise rates and to charge duties on coal and tonnage at Colchester's port, the Hythe. The income thus raised was devoted to the twin purposes of improving the navigation of the river Colne between the Hythe and Wivenhoe, and paving, lighting, cleansing and improving the town.[19]

From an early stage the Commissioners devoted the majority of their income to this latter purpose. An expanding programme of street lighting was maintained, pavements were laid, roads repaired and old, dangerous, or inconvenient buildings – some might call them picturesque – were removed. By this means much of the old Middle Row in the High Street was destroyed, and the last of the medieval gateways, St Botolph's, pulled down.[20] More significantly for our purposes, urged on by one of the more remarkable figures of Regency Colchester, the Borough Chamberlain, Benjamin Strutt, the Commissioners closed a number of old wells. Questions of hygiene may have governed this decision and with the increase of wheeled transport, King Coel's Pump, one of the first to go, might have been termed an obstacle. But it is also worth seeking an explanation from Thomas Cromwell whose *History of Colchester* was compiled during 1824. Cromwell was a commercial writer with little previous knowledge of the town. His history he lifted almost word for word from Morant, but for current events he relied on leading citizens. Five were sufficiently significant to be named in the preface. All five had acted as Commissioners; one of them was Colchester Agent to the Waterworks Company; another was Ben Strutt. Under their guidance Cromwell is full of praise for the new Waterworks, and says of the removal of King Coel's Pump:

> "The necessity for this and nearly all such Public Pumps in Colchester has ceased to exist since the establishment of the waterworks".[21]

How far this judgement was justified, only time would tell. In any event the interaction between the Waterworks and the Commissioners, both of them protected and circumscribed by legislation, was to be a recurring theme of the next 50 years.

2

1840-1850: Railways and Public Health

With Dodd's waterworks Colchester entered the Victorian Age, experiencing in its own small way that growth of population that was one of the most striking features of the century. In 1801 the population had been calculated at 11,520. By 1841 it had risen to 17,790.[1] These additional 6,000 souls were housed, not by any expansion of the town's perimeter, but by greater population density in the centre. More people were crammed into ageing housing, new properties were built on garden grounds, and main roads like North Hill sprouted dark courts and alleys in which the poor eked out their overcrowded lives. The built-up area of 1841 was little changed from that of late medieval times. Indeed, with the exception of the long line of Magdalen Street extending to the Hythe and East Hill extending to the river, a large percentage of the town still lay within the Roman walls.

Even when, from the 1840s, new houses were built and new streets laid out, further problems arose. St Mary's Terrace, the beginning of middle-class housing along Lexden Road, deposited its sewage downhill to a cesspit which, it was claimed, would contaminate the Chiswell Meadow water supply.[2] A major new housing area, built on Cant's nursery ground and extending to South Street, made no general provision for its drainage which, seeking lower ground, formed a stagnant pond a quarter of an acre in size, most of it, with singular inappropriateness, covering the back garden of Dr. Churchill, the town's coroner. Using his influence, Churchill understandably made a fuss, but here he came up against a familiar contemporary impasse. The Commissioners did not possess the power to build a drain over private ground, while the Turnpike Trust denied that the drainage beyond that point was their responsibility. Three years later the pond was still there.[3]

Colchester was discovering, like the rest of Britain, the pressing need for urban sanitation. During the 1840s this became a major national issue and to its leaders a moral and administrative crusade. A

DR. JOHN CHURCHILL, Colchester's coroner, viewing with impotent displeasure the flooding of his Crouch Street garden by the drainage from Colchester's first housing estate.

string of official and unofficial publications, headed by Edwin Chadwick's *Report on the Sanitary Condition of the Labouring Population*, revealed insanitary horrors in our major cities that made St Mary's cesspit and Churchill's pond appear like minor irritants.[4] National pressure groups arose, notably the Health of Towns Association, whose publicity bulletins appeared in the Colchester press, and whose London Secretary twice addressed moderately attended meetings in the town.[5] The campaign reached a climax with the passing of the Public Health Act of 1848, a measure which historians now regard as something of a failure. How did these national events affect affairs in Colchester? In fact they were largely overshadowed by another contemporary issue – the coming of the railway.

East Anglia was not well served by its first railway promoters. The Eastern Counties Railway, to whom this privilege fell, scored high in that league table of financial chicanery, legal elusiveness and gangland tactics towards rivals that too often accompanied the advance of the iron road. The rapacity of promoters too often overruled the interests of shareholders, let alone the interests of the public, while Parliament at best offered an uneasy restraining hand.[6]

Authorised in 1836 to build from London to Norwich via Ipswich, the Eastern Counties spent £2.5 million and took seven years to reach Colchester. Construction costs alone for these 51 miles were over £1.5 million, more than the estimates for the entire line to Norwich. On top of this, vast sums had been paid in compensation to wealthy landowners (some might call these bribes) to silence any opposition to the scheme that might jeopardise its Parliamentary approval. This had been deemed necessary in order to forestall the Eastern Counties' greater fear of being outbid by the Northern and Eastern Railway who planned a rival line to Norwich via Cambridge.[7]

At long last the first train limped into Colchester on March 18th 1843, two days after an official opening ceremony when up to 2,000 people had waited in vain for its arrival. Even so, the journey was only

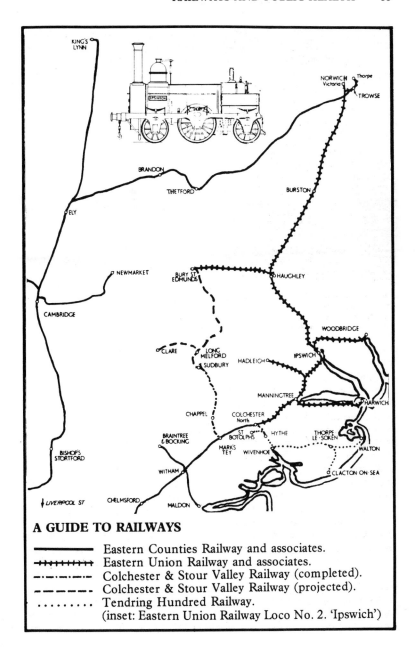

A GUIDE TO RAILWAYS

——————————— Eastern Counties Railway and associates.
+++++++++++ Eastern Union Railway and associates.
—·—·—·—·— Colchester & Stour Valley Railway (completed).
— — — — —· Colchester & Stour Valley Railway (projected).
· · · · · · · · Tendring Hundred Railway.
(inset: Eastern Union Railway Loco No. 2. 'Ipswich')

just made, one of the Directors volunteering to walk under the timber viaduct at Lexden as the train edged cautiously over it.[18] In one sense the railway almost passed Colchester by. Allegedly from engineering problems, but mainly because of the high prices demanded for land on its western approaches, Colchester acquired a meagre and windswept terminus, three quarters of a mile from the town centre, inconveniently sited beyond the steep slope of North Hill and the questionable stability of North Bridge. In terms of a goods service for Colchester merchants this hardly boded well.

At Colchester's North Station the railway halted. The Eastern Counties, financially extended, refused to go further. In vain did those Ipswich merchants who had backed the project from the start protest and seek legal injunctions against the company. Norwich meanwhile, tired of waiting, launched their own line, the Norwich and Brandon, westwards, inviting both the Eastern Counties and the Northern and Eastern to extend to meet it. Such risky competition was swiftly eliminated when in January 1844 the Eastern Counties took over the Northern and Eastern line. They now controlled both approaches to Norwich, that via Cambridge and that which ended at Colchester. Worse still, to the dismay of Ipswich, it emerged that this eastern route, when and if it was extended, was planned to by-pass Ipswich altogether.[9]

Faced with this crisis Ipswich rallied behind the energetic leadership of John Chevallier Cobbold, brewer, banker and M.P. for the town. Conscious of the Eastern Counties' claim that the line to Ipswich "presented difficulties that were almost insuperable", Cobbold consulted Peter Schuyler Bruff.

Bruff had a colourful pedigree. Son of a Portsmouth naval engineer who had been a personal friend of Nelson, his grandparent's family, the Schuylers, had been pioneer settlers of America. Drawn into the heroic age of railway building, Bruff had been Assistant Engineer to Joseph Locke, himself a pupil of George Stephenson, and the man responsible for the Eastern Counties' slow and expensive advance to Colchester. Locke's contribution to railway construction was the realisation that the increasing power of locomotives could cope with sharper gradients and curves than had hitherto been countenanced. In this he was followed by Bruff, whose proposed line to Ipswich followed a route which crossed the Dedham Vale on the skew, with gradients along the side, and slid into Ipswich beside the Orwell in order to avoid the greater expense of travelling by viaduct or embankment straight across these obstacles.[10] A Parliamentary struggle with a rival Eastern Counties scheme was won and the Eastern Union Railway was launched on cash raised by Cobbold and his Ipswich colleagues. In June 1846 the inaugural train, supervised by Bruff and carrying Cobbold and his fellow Directors, arrived at Colchester to meet a train from London carrying the Eastern Counties chairman, the

The arrival of the first train from Ipswich at Colchester North Station, June 11th 1846. The foreground is dominated by the Victoria Hotel (later an Asylum for Idiots). The artist has taken a generous view of the height and distance of the town centre.

notorious 'railway king', George Hudson, also chairman of the Midland Railway, and by now recognised as the most dynamic railway promoter in the country. Even though the contractors had caused great offence by working on the Sabbath, and even though Bruff's curves and gradients were to be the curse of high speed trains a century later, the completion of the Ipswich line at reasonable cost was a great triumph for the resident engineer, himself now an Ipswich resident.[11]

These events were less welcome at Colchester. The avowed aim of the Eastern Union was not only to establish a direct link with London, but to win for Ipswich and its substantial new wet docks a prize which Colchester had previously claimed – control via a branch line to Hadleigh over the trade of south Suffolk and, via a branch from Mannigtree to Harwich, over the Stour valley as well. For this reason the Colchester community, particularly those merchants whose coal yards, timber stacks and maltings were centred on the Hythe, had supported the rival Eastern Counties' proposal of a line from Colchester to Norwich direct, passing Ipswich by.[12] That battle now lost, the Hythe merchants turned to a much bolder strategy. In this they were led by William Hawkins, the town's wealthiest and most forceful businessman, who with his brother, Charles, owned the entire eastern wharfage of the Hythe; their extensive timber yards, then as now, dominating that side of the river. For some years Hawkins had been urging the need for an improvement in the tidal navigation for, left to itself, the Hythe inexorably silted up. Consequently, most bulk cargoes had to be unloaded at Wivenhoe and brought up river at high water by lighters, an expensive and time-consuming business. Those larger ships which did attempt this hazardous journey risked the possibility of getting stuck on the shoals which constantly built up on bends in the river or, worse still, of being marooned at the Hythe for days on end as high tides got progressively lower.[13]

Even before the line from Ipswich opened, Hawkins approached Peter Bruff. The proposals that emerged from the consultations of these two men were ambitious and far-reaching. Essentially two related projects were put forward, the first of which swiftly became a reality. A new railway company, the Stour Valley Railway, was launched, to join Colchester with Sudbury, then standing at the head of the Stour Navigation. This railway was built in two phases. Firstly, and most urgently, the Hythe quayside, itself some 2.25 miles by road from North Station, was linked by rail with the Eastern Union line to the north of the town. Secondly, a branch line to Sudbury was commenced at Marks Tey, five miles to the west of Colchester on the Eastern Counties line. The Hythe and Stour valley would thus be directly linked by rail, and the Stour valley trade secured. The confidence with which this prospect was regarded was underlined by the new railway's dealings with the existing Stour Navigation Company which ran barge traffic down the river to Manningtree. The Directors of the Navigation, having been persuaded to take up shares in the railway on the understanding that their Company would be purchased, asked for £30,000 only to receive a derisory counter-offer of £1,000 and the suggestion that they should like it or lump it.[14]

The second part of the Bruff/Hawkins scheme was not new. Indeed, it had been on the table since the railway first crept towards Colchester and Bruff had been – briefly – a resident of the town. It was a bold and expensive plan to overcome the Hythe's permanent shortage of water by cutting a separate ship canal to Wivenhoe and installing a dam at Rowhedge to turn the river up to the Hythe into a still-water basin. Colchester would thus become, like Ipswich, a 24-hour port.[15]

While the benefit of these measures to Colchester is self-evident, they should also be seen against the broad strategy of the Eastern Union Railway of which Bruff was both a shareholder and managing engineer. These were the closing years of 'Railway Mania'. The Stour Valley Railway was but part of a wider national picture in which the alleged profits of the first generation of railway companies, the taste for blood their promoters had acquired, and the apparent readiness of the middle classes to invest in anything, produced an unholy scramble to complete the main outline of the national railway network before any rival company did.

The central figure in this drama, George Hudson, by now at the height of his fame and reputation, was, as we have seen, also Chairman of the Eastern Counties. During 1846, besides seeking to salvage its creaking operations, he was also using it to support his own Midland Railway in its bid to secure a second major north-south route in Britain. Front runner for this prize was the Midland's rival, the Great Northern Railway, and part of Hudson's strategy involved a bid - ultimately unsuccessful - to extend the Eastern Counties into the industrial heart of England.[16]

While this contest of Titans was proceeding, Bruff's Eastern Union had not been inactive. Long before the Ipswich to Colchester line was completed, Parliamentary approval was secured for a subsidiary company, the Bury and Ipswich, linking those two towns. This company in turn secured approval to run a line from a midpoint between Bury and Ipswich to Norwich. The Eastern Counties monopoly to London could now be broken, and that by a more direct route. Cobbold and Bruff, fêted by the Norwich city fathers, were quietly establishing a new centre of railway gravity, linked as they now would be with the railway network developing in Norfolk.[17]

PETER SCHUYLER BRUFF, engineer, railway builder and resort developer, anticipates with inner confidence the legal devices he has planned in order to confound his enemies.

Pondering these things, Bruff might well reflect that though their relationship was currently cordial, the Eastern Union and Eastern Counties might soon be at war, once the rival route to Norwich was completed. Were this to happen, the town of Colchester was peculiarly situated at the very point where the lines of the two companies met en route to London. The Hythe loop can thus be seen as an offer that could not be refused, coaxing Colchester into the Ipswich camp. Not only did the loop feed onto the Eastern Union line, but, from its incorporation, the Stour Valley carried the option of a later lease to the Bury and Ipswich, a tacit undertaking to bale it out in case of trouble, or to assimilate it should it get ambitions of its own. For it was also true, as everybody realised, that the Stour Valley would run over five miles of the Eastern Counties line in order to branch off to

Sudbury. If any future war got too hot, the Stour Valley might play a dangerous game, and woo the Eastern Counties. For even while the Hythe loop was being built, Bruff and Hawkins were eying the possibilities of doing what the Eastern Counties had failed to do: to break into the industrial midlands by extending the Stour Valley line from Sudbury to Cambridge, hitherto the Eastern Counties' stronghold. However distanced by questions of capital and Parliamentary approval, this was a glittering prospect to the wharfholders at the Hythe, and it might not hurt their sponsorship by the Eastern Union to flirt a little with the other side.[18]

Now what have all these devious railway conspiracies to do with the Colchester Waterworks? Simply that railway politics brought Peter Bruff to Colchester, and that the last years of Railway Mania coincided as we shall now see with the great public health crusade.

Bruff's second proposal, the ship canal, had a less happy time. Such a major development clearly involved the Commissioners, the established guardians of the Navigation. They in turn would have to go to Parliament to seek the approval of the Lords of the Admiralty and to raise the £50,000 necessary for the scheme. Immediately there were problems. Although Colchester and the Commissioners were in general enthusiastic, the Admiralty's investigators argued that the proposed dam at Rowhedge was technically unsound, while a still-water basin would not only deprive the channel of the scouring action of the river and the retreating tide, but would deprive Colchester of its main sewage outlet. The winding channel to Wivenhoe might still silt up, and not with mud alone. Bruff therefore put up a revised plan in 1847 that involved a still-water basin and a wet dock confined to the Hythe. By now however growing hostility to the plan came not just from the Admiralty but from Colchester itself. Increasingly it was noted, particularly by John Taylor, editor and proprietor of the Colchester-based *Essex Standard*, that the promoters of the Stour Valley Railway and of the Hythe basin tended to be the same people – the private owners of the Hythe quayside. Might not the improvement of the navigation at public expense largely benefit the private businesses of a few men, notably the Hawkins brothers?[19]

These and other criticisms, not least the prospect of the expense involved, led to the defeat of the entire measure. The whole fiasco cost over £5,500, £1,311 of it in fees to Peter Bruff. Not for the last time in Colchester, private Acts of Parliament were somewhat discredited, while the smouldering hostility between John Taylor and the Hawkins brothers eventually led, on other grounds, to the publication by Hawkins of a rival newspaper with the avowed aim of putting the *Essex Standard* out of business.[20]

The 1847 Channel Bill did however have one constructive consequence. Given the expense of a Parliamentary Bill, the opportunity was also taken to reconstitute and strengthen the

Commissioners in their dual role as administrators of the port and guardians of the town's environment. In more ways than one, sewage disposal and the river were to remain linked. The new Commissioners were to be henceforth an elected body of twenty-four with seats reserved for major ship owners at the Hythe, instead of being open as

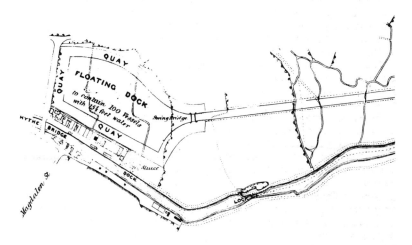

Part of Bruff's 1842 plans for a wet dock at the Hythe fed by a ship canal from Wivenhoe.

before to some 200 leading ratepayers. They were thus to epitomise, as their subsequent actions were to show, that tension between public benefit and private gain that is the underlying theme of this our tale. For while the elective principle imposed on the Commissioners the onus of accountability, elections soon became almost a formality and the twenty-four Commissioners close to a self-perpetuating oligarchy of leading citizens with economic interests in the town. Consequently, even after 1847, expenditure upon the river or modification of the channel dues, issues which like the tide itself ebbed to and fro over the next 40 years, were always likely to receive more support from Hythe merchants and ship owners, and more opposition from those who depended entirely upon the railway for their business. At the same time there were also those like John Taylor among the Commissioners who from inclination or occupation might claim to speak solely for the public good, rather than the economic underpinning of their own business. Others again argued that these two objectives were not incompatible; that the businesses that they ran generated employment in the town; that an improved river, if only by a multiplier effect, ultimately benefited the whole community. The feasibility of bringing bulk goods into the Hythe could also deter the railway companies from introducing exorbitant freight rates, an imposition which those towns confronted by a railway monopoly were soon to experience, and which the builders of the Hythe loop were already seeking to exploit. Indeed this was to be one of the Hythe's chief functions during the remainder of the Victorian period. But while it might be easy to demonstrate the ecconomic advantages of improving the channel, it was less easy to make the same claim for public health.[21]

The reconstituted Commissioners also received enlarged powers – though subsequent events were to suggest that these were not large enough. They were now able to levy a two shilling rate, and their borrowing powers were raised to £10,000. Model clauses, prepared by the government, were adopted for their new Act, including compulsory powers to lay sewers over private ground, a facility that would at last make possible the removal of Churchill's pond. Indeed the evidence given at the government enquiry that preceded their Bill made very clear the task that lay ahead.

Despite its convenient location on a hill sloping down to the river, the drainage system of Colchester was haphazard and random. As was common at the time, sewage and surface drainage intermingled. Five main sewers, many of them open ditches, fed by gravity into the river. The most important of these was the ancient stream rising from a spring near St Botolph's Corner and running diagonally past Priory Street to reach the river via the aptly named Brook Street. Along its verges lay a number of allotments and market gardens whose owners deliberately dammed its course to harvest its free but powerful contents as a fertiliser. Since few homes boasted water closets, most human sewage accumulated in outhouse privies and cesspits to be emptied at none-too-frequent intervals by scavengers or 'night-soil men' who, fortified with hard spirits, toured the town at night shovelling the contents of cesspits into special carts which were hopefully, though not always, watertight. As dawn broke they wended their way into the country to sell their reeking cargoes to local farmers, though not before stopping on the town's perimeter for some refreshment after their night's labours. Two favourite rendezvous were The Globe pub in North Street where drowsy early risers might be startled into sharper consciousness by encountering the leaking carts, and the field beside East Bridge where up to six teams might assemble for breakfast and an exchange of professional news.[22]

So long as muck was brass, there was a vested interest in resisting its removal by the agencies of public health. When cholera struck Colchester in 1834 owners of dung heaps physically defended their stock-in-trade from interference by the Commissioners. Great enthusiasm therefore accompanied the suggestion of the Public Health Movement that local authorities might themselves enter the field and market town sewage at a profit. This view was held with especial tenacity by Edwin Chadwick, the sanitary king, now at the height of his national reputation. He personally supervised an experiment in which a steam barge pounded along a canal spraying liquid sewage through a hose on to adjacent fields. Such commercial inventiveness was not without its local exponents. At Chelmsford, members of the Marriage family claimed to be making a profit from the sale of sewage, while at Tiptree the unorthodox figure of Alderman Mechi, a wealthy City merchant whose hobby of experimental agriculture was rapidly becoming an obsession, loudly proclaimed the merits of the scheme. Mechi was already a nationally known figure, partly from his strident articles in the press, partly from his lavish and well-publicised entertainment of leading public figures from the farming world, who gathered every year at his Tiptree farm to tour its installations and feast at his expense. Chadwick himself attended on several occasions.[23]

In Colchester the initiative was taken by Joseph Cooke, a leading citizen and ex-mayor, who, setting out to exploit the commercial possibilities of town sewage felt it necessary to resign his seat as a Commissioner because of a potential conflict of interests. Unfortunately for Joseph Cooke, and arguably the nation's health, the mass importation from the 1850s of guano from seabird islands off the coast of Peru knocked the bottom out of the sewage market. Though essentially produced in much the same way, guano proved not only distinctly easier to handle but, even after its long sea journey, far cheaper in the market. Before long Joseph Cooke abandoned his experiment, and once more joined the body of Commissioners, though the phantom of profits from processed sewage continued to tempt and disappoint its advocates for three decades.[24]

Forced to accept that enviromental health could not be achieved without expense, the Commissioners soon realised that the cautious expansion of their borrowing powers and their ability to raise a two shil-

JOSEPH COOKE (1795-1864), mayor and woolstapler, reflects glumly on his failure to market town sewage at a profit. The finished product was, he protested, "altogether too liquid".

ling rate under the new Act were both woefully inadequate. Consequently, their first major undertaking, a unified drainage system for the town, had to be phased over seven years. Moreover, the project got off to a distinctly bad start, partly as a consequence of accepting the cheapest tender, partly as a reflection of the limited technical knowledge available in even so large a market town as Colchester. As the excavations for the drainage passed down St John's Street, disaster struck. Digging too deep into the sandy soil the sides began to give way and several labourers fought for their lives to struggle from the engulfing soil. Two were buried alive. Subsequent enquiries revealed that the men who had contracted to complete the pipe-laying were regarded as so inexperienced that they were regularly supervised by the Commissioners' own surveyor, acting in effect as foreman of the works.[25]

If the Commissioners thus made heavy weather with the drainage, they had greater problems with that other aspect of public health, the water supply. Here they faced a private company, itself protected by Parliamentary powers, whose services, despite its initial proud claims, were now sadly wanting. Firstly, the waterworks' mains only extended to some 15 streets on the west side of the town, representing well under half of the built-up area. Secondly, within these streets water was only supplied to those householders willing to meet the costs of installing and maintaining their own connecting pipes and paying an annual water rate of about thirty shillings for a substantial house. Thirdly, water was only pumped by the engines through the mains for a few hours on three days a week, and never on a Sunday. Sizeable domestic storage cisterns and considerable restraint in their use was therefore essential if water was to be available on demand. Thus were perhaps 600 households supplied, somewhat over 15% of the total in the borough. Even this privileged minority frequently found during the summer months that the water stored in their cisterns became so unpleasant to the taste that they resorted to the practice of the poor who purchased water by the bucket from a mobile water cart. Indeed there was growing misgiving about even the initial purity of the Waterworks' supply. Not only was there the risk of contamination from the Lexden Road cesspit, but the standing reservoirs at the Balkerne Works, open to the heavens, provided an inviting environment for a host of aquatic life. A strident campaign in the *Ipswich Express*, the mouthpiece of radical opinion in Colchester, compiled from its readers' letters a formidable check-list of amphibia allegedly delivered via the Waterworks' mains. Even if some of these had more probably bred in the domestic cisterns, it hardly reduced the sense of concern they raised.[26]

It is significant that these criticisms were intially voiced in a Liberal newspaper. As the party of protest and reform, Liberalism was more likely to produce supporters of the Public Health campaign. In a body like the Commisssioners, which successfully avoided party bickering, such political identification need not be a drawback. This however was not the case in the Borough Council. Here partisan behaviour was extreme, and it is fundamental to an understanding of our narrative to appreciate that nothing of a public nature took place in the 19th-century Colchester without there being political overtones. Whenever Mr X expressed an opinion on any public matter, his political disposition was inevitably in the back of his hearers' minds. Partly this was a consequence of the relatively small business élite within the town. The old adage that everyone knew everyone else's business extended to political persuasions too, and so long as the franchise was neither secret nor universal, political neutrality was practically unknown. This was reinforced by the fact that political affiliation was increasingly a product of a yet more vital area of life. Business partnerships, social life and marriages were all governed by the fundamental fact that the leadership of the Conservative Party was entirely Anglican, while their Liberal counterparts were, with the exception of a few gentry, invariably members of the town's very active noncomformist churches. This religious divide permeated all aspects of the community, in a town which according to one calculation had a higher incidence of church attendance then any other of its size in England.[27]

Several Liberal names were active in the public health issue, but by far the most important was John Bawtree Harvey. Significantly, Harvey was both a journalist and Ipswich-born. He came to Colchester in 1837 to launch a Liberal newspaper in the town, turning the old *Colchester Gazette* into the *Essex and Suffolk Times*. Within two years he was editing no less than three newspapers including, significantly, the newly promoted *Ipswich Express*. All three newspapers however ran at a loss, partly because Harvey's detailed reports of Chartist activities offended many respectable subscribers. In 1841 the papers were sold, though the *Ipswich Express*, as we have seen, continued its Liberal stance. Notwithstanding the political and financial setbacks that this entailed, Harvey was to remain a key figure in the town. A lifetime of service to Colchester lay ahead. If only in terms of hours devoted to the cause, Harvey was, quite simply, the town's most outstanding public servant in the 19th century.[28]

The emergence of Harvey as champion of the sanitary cause in 1847 was linked not only to the national movement, but to the resurgence of the Liberal presence in the borough. In 1847, almost to their own surprise, the Liberals won one of Colchester's Parliamentary seats. This had a carry-over effect at the Borough Council elections later that year when the Liberals won five seats in a hitherto totally Conservative Council. One of these five was Harvey. In 1848 Harvey and his friends also stood for the Commissioners and were elected amidst Conservative complaints, rare for that body, that there were political undertones to their intent.[29]

Harvey was therefore fortunate that a leading Conservative had also come forward in the sanitary cause. Dr Williams was not only a senior physician in the town, the only one to be elected to the Commissioners, but he was also a Conservative alderman and, from November 1849, mayor of Colchester. Early that year in response to the allegations in the *Ipswich Express*, he wrote a series of letters to the *Essex Standard*, sure of the support of its editor, John Taylor. In them he attempted a detailed review of the water supply of the town, coming down heavily against the Waterworks Company for its inadequate provision. What, he asked, rhetorically, would subscribers think of a gas company which only supplied gas on three days a week? Stung by such attacks, the Waterworks Company issued a handbill undertaking to begin a daily supply. There is reason to believe, however, that this promise was not honoured.[30]

DR EDWARD WILLIAMS (1808-1877), a man of wide reading and oversize greatcoats, was for 40 years Physician to the Essex and Colchester Hospital, though not always to their satisfaction. However his contribution to the Public Health Movement was less equivocal.

With Williams thus occupied in the *Standard*, Harvey in the columns of the *Express* initiated an attack on that other source of water, the public wells, the undoubted responsibility of the Borough Council. If anything, this proved to be an even greater indictment, revealing neglect of upkeep, encroachment by private individuals, wanton pollution and deliberate diversion from the public use by both the Council and the Commissioners. Of 20 public pumps or wells that had been in full use up to 30 years previously, and most of which had served the burgesses since medieval times, only seven were in satisfactory condition and current use. Significantly, most of these were on the east side of the town, where the pipes of the Waterworks had never penetrated. A few examples of abuse will suffice to illustrate the total picture. On North Hill three public springs had been directed into the sewer and covered over as part of a road improvement scheme. The Stanwell or Stonewell (in Stanwell Street) was regularly polluted by fish hawkers washing out their baskets and was used in such quantities by the Commissioners for watering the roads that the

COLCHESTER
WATER WORKS.

The Water Works Company, with a view to the convenience of, and for the purpose of affording (if possible) a better supply of Water to their Tenants, have made arrangements for a daily service.

In refutation of the statements that have recently appeared as to the Quality of the Water, the Directors have to state that it has been proved by an Analysis, made by an Eminent Professor, to be Pure, and of a Superior description.

The Directors therefore conclude that the impurities alluded to in such statements arise from want of proper Emptying and Cleansing the domestic Butts and Cisterns, which the Directors hope will not be neglected in future.

With an anxious desire to afford the greatest accommodation to their Tenants, the Directors feel compelled to caution them against abuses which are detrimental to the Company's interests, and to express their determination to carry out to the fullest extent the provisions of their Act of Parliament, against all persons who are in the habit of allowing others not Tenants to use the Water, or to suffer the same to run to waste.

A REWARD OF 40s.

Will be paid by the Company's Agent, to any person giving such inform-ation and evidence as may lead to the Conviction of Offenders.

By Order of the Directors,

F. G. ABELL,

COLCHESTER, 1849.   *Agent.*

FENTON, PRINTER AND BOOKSELLER, HIGH STREET, COLCHESTER.

The poster issued by the Waterworks in 1849 following the attacks of Bawtree Harvey and Dr. Williams. Note the name at the bottom for future reference.

poor of the vicinity had to fetch their water by pails from the Abbey
Well set 200 yards away by the old wall of St John's Abbey. Finally, the
thickly populated area of the Hythe depended for its supply on water
piped from springs to the south. This supply had been severely
disrupted by Colchester's first artesian well, sunk over 30 years before
to supply the stables of the military barracks established in Colchester
during the Napoleonic Wars. The barracks had long since gone; the
disrupted water supply remained.[31]

Reading this catalogue of abuse, one is forced to conclude that the
great population growth of the past 50 years and the failure of these
traditional sources to keep pace had left the poor of Colchester,
notably those living on the mile-long road from St Botolph's to the
Hythe, less well supplied with water than they had ever been before.
To them the Waterworks were an irrelevance. Not only were most of
them beyond the reach of its mains, but installation and maintenance
costs were far beyond the poor man's pocket. On the other hand, the
fact that the majority of the inoperative wells lay within that area of
the town served by the Waterworks leaves the uneasy suspicion that
the provision of even a three-day supply to the comfortable classes
who governed the town had encouraged their neglect of ancient rights
and community facilities.

Having thus alerted the public in the best Benthamite manner with
this review of deficiency and abuse, Harvey and Williams now pressed
their case on the two relevant public bodies, the Borough Council and
the Commissioners. They could take great encouragement from
national events. An apparently major victory for the sanitary cause had
now been achieved with the 1848 Public Health Act, setting up a
General Board of Health, an almost autonomous central body to be
run by Edwin Chadwick. Below the Board of Health towns could at the
request of one tenth of the ratepayers establish a Local Board of
Health which, in case of a borough like Colchester, would be identical
with the Borough Council. They would then receive large powers to
implement a comprehensive sanitary programme upon lines long
since outlined by Edwin Chadwick. This programme owed much to the
popular medical opinion of the day that disease somehow arose
spontaneously from putrid matter. With the germ theory of disease
still to be conclusively established, this was a not unhelpful diagnosis,
based, as it was, on considerable evidence that disease was more
prevalent where bad smells accompanied decaying matter. Chadwick
however disposed of all nuances by the bald claim that "all smell is, if
it be intense, immediate, acute disease". On this basis the main object
of the sanitary movement should be to remove all smell and all
deposits of decaying matter. First in line were the contents of cesspits.
Chadwick advocated the universal installation of a new type of oval
ceramic sewer pipe through which domestic sewage as well as surface
drainage would be flushed by fresh water, instead of lying stagnant in

the brick sewers and open ditches of the day. These proposals were ambitious, even visionary, and were scarcely to be realised in Chadwick's long lifetime. Above all, they depended for success not only on new sewer pipes, but on a constant supply of piped water to flush them out. Colchester at least was committed, however slowly, to new sewers. Would it now adopt the Public Health Act and compel the Waterworks Company to provide an improved, let alone a 24-hour supply?[32]

For Chadwick's logic was no longer the only influence at work. In 1848 the second major outbreak of cholera spread across Europe and landed in our ports reaching its peak in the summer of 1849. In a now classic example of misguided dogmatism Chadwick had all London's sewers flushed into the Thames which was for many the sole source of their domestic water supply. In his defence it should be noted that Chadwick's action had the support of many doctors, since medical opinion was not yet aware that cholera is mainly transmitted by drinking water or eating food contaminated by the excrement of those already suffering from the disease.[33]

DIPHTHERIA   SCROFULA   CHOLERA

A cartoon recording the 'great stink' of 1856 shows Father Thames presenting the City of London with his offspring, Diphtheria, Scrofula and Cholera.

Spurred into action by this most virulent of killers, Parliament rushed through a Nuisance Removal Act requiring every Board of Guardians, the local custodians of the Workhouse, to appoint an official to search out and remove all accumulations of filth in their district and, by a house-to-house search, to check any outbreak of the disease. It is typical of the ambiguity of early health legislation, as well as the amateur skills of its local interpreters, that in Colchester the Board of Guardians proceeded to appoint their aptly named Inspector of Nuisances when not only did the Commissioners already employ such an official, but, as they belatedly discovered, under the terms of the new Act, they, not the Guardians, were the more appropriate administering body. There was even serious discussion among the Commissioners as to whether *their* Inspector of Nuisances was under any obligation to act upon information supplied by the Guardian's Inspector.[34]

In September 1849 the worst cholera epidemic in our history reached its peak in London, with 6,644 deaths that month from the disease. There was also in September a cholera death in Colchester. In October Harvey's report on the wells came before a special meeting of the Borough Council. It clearly demonstrated that the poor would never achieve domestic cleanliness so long as water was so difficult to obtain. With untypical speed a resolution was carried inviting the Commissioners, with the Council's full support, to secure an adequate water supply for the town, if necessary by adopting the 1848 Act.[35] Within a week the Commissioners met, agreed and set up their own Committee to meet jointly with that of the Corporation.

Two months of silence followed. A cholera outbreak did not develop in the town. In January the Committee reported to the Commissioners:

"that the powers of the local Act for supplying the town with water be fully carried into effect before any other powers are applied for".[36]

Behind this bald statement on which the press, earlier so strident, made no comment, lay the defeat of the Harvey/Williams initiative, and the end, so far as Colchester was concerned, of the Public Health Act of 1848. Why was this?

Doubtless the retreat of King Cholera played a part, although there was yet no certainty that the epidemic would not revive. There was also misgiving, even voiced by a leading Liberal, that the General Board of Health represented the unwarranted intrusion of central government into local affairs. Finally, given the Commissioners' recent experience with an Act of Parliament, there was the question of expense, always a powerful deterrent to action, especially while the town's economy was still less than flourishing. Not only had there been a further decline in the trade at the Hythe, but the town's role as a market was not helped by the apprehension still felt by local agriculturalists at the repeal of the Corn Laws in 1846.[37] Hence the Joint Committee's official conclusion: that not only was there already an Act of Parliament requiring the Waterworks Company to supply the town, but, with considerable disturbance and no small expense, the town had but recently reconstituted the Commissioners with power to require the Waterworks Company to honour that Act.

However, if this was the real intention of their statement, little evidence survives of any move by the Commissioners to follow it up. On the contrary, when at their next meeting Harvey pressed for further investigations, he was greeted as if he were reviving an issue already resolved. Surely, argued one leading Conservative, the matter could now be left until the summer? Harvey, however, got his extended enquiry approved, and in June produced another detailed report, tabulating the lack of water supply to the poorer districts of the town and recommending the provision of several storage reservoirs in the worst places at the Commissioners' expense.[38] But by now the national cholera epidemic had totally passed, the Guardian's Inspector of Nuisances had ceased his duties, and despite his final report, impressive for its record of bulk cleansing, and disturbing for its evidence of abuses still existing, the Commissioners saw no need to replace him at their own expense.[39] It therefore seems unlikely that anything would have come of Harvey's reservoir proposals, even if circumstances had not suddenly changed. For early in 1851 the news broke that the Colchester Waterworks had been purchased by William Hawkins and Peter Bruff.[40]

Eastern Union Railway, Loco: No.12.

3

1850-1860: Mr Harvey Proposes

Both at the time and in later years, it was implied that the purchase
of the waterworks by Bruff and Hawkins, like the earlier promotion of
the ship canal, had been done as much in the public interest as in the
pursuit of profit. The existing waterworks, the local trade directory
declared, were "a profitless speculation", while an anonymous letter in
the *Essex Standard*, which could have been ghosted by Hawkins,
rejoiced that:

> "the Waterworks is no longer in the hands of a Board of
> Directors in London looking for a dividend only, but in the
> hands of local gentlemen and that able engineer, Peter
> Bruff . . ."

whose many merits are then listed, including that of being the first
subscriber to the town's museum. Clearly, after the affair of the ship
canal, some image adjustment was necessary.[1]
    There was also the question of the Stour Valley Railway. This had
been launched, you will recall, as two projects, the Hythe loop and the
Marks Tey to Sudbury line. The former was rapidly completed; the
latter made negligible progress. Then, in 1847, 1,000 men were put
to work, constructing a permanent way that would accommodate a
double line to Sudbury. This expensive gesture was explained when,
soon afterwards, the Stour Valley Company sought and obtained
Parliamentary approval to extend the line beyond Sudbury to Long
Melford and from there west to Clare and north to Bury St Edmunds,
which was, as Bruff pointed out, by 20 miles a nearer route from
London to Bury than the existing Ipswich route. Clearly what had been
originally projected as a single-track branch line was rapidly becoming
a major trunk route, for the other extension, the Clare turn-off, could,
like the line to Bury, fulfil Bruff's promise of a rail link from the Hythe
to Cambridge and from there to the industrial Midlands.
    At first sight these proposals appear a direct threat to the

Bruff's Chappel Viaduct strides the Colne Valley on 32 arches, some 75 feet above the valley floor. Among its 400 navvies, all formidable men, was Tom Sayers, all-England champion, the last of the bare-fist prize fighters.

Company's godfather, the Eastern Union. However, an alternative explanation was brought out by awkward questions asked at the Parliamentary Enquiry by counsel for the opposing landowners. For when the Stour Valley spokesman refused to answer how long 1,000 men had been employed, and were to be employed, and how much track they had laid so far, counsel recalled that on a previous application for an extension into Norfolk, the Eastern Union had employed 1,000 men and had promptly withdrawn them after application had been granted. The aim of the Stour Valley, he argued, was merely to block off the route to anyone else. Since this was a common tactic of the day, not unknown to the Eastern Counties itself, there may be some substance in the accusation and therefore less threat to the Eastern Union.[2]

But if true, this was an expensive deceit. The demands of providing for a double line to Sudbury delayed completion and multiplied costs. This was particularly serious given Bruff's decision to cross the Colne Valley at the village of Chappel by a giant 32-arch viaduct, the largest and highest in the east of England. Consuming seven million bricks and the labour of 40 horses and 400 men, it was still incomplete when matters reached a crisis in September 1848.[3] Needing to raise an extra £83,000, the directors resolved to press for the earlier undertaking of the Bury and Ipswich, i.e. the Eastern Union, formally to take over the Stour Valley on a 999 year lease. This produced protests from both sets of shareholders. In the case of the Stour Valley, the protesters were mostly Colchester investors and mostly, as it happened, Colchester Liberals. Accusations began to fly of a sort familiar in the age of railway speculation : the Stour Valley prospectus, they pointed out, had promised 10% but was now to be leased to the Eastern Union at a fixed 5%. The same prospectus contained the name of a leading banker who had in fact purchased only one share. More seriously, a number of large shareholders had not paid up on their shares, while some of the promoters, including apparently Bruff, had bought their shares with money loaned by Richard Sanderson, the broker and Conservative M.P. for Colchester so rudely dispossessed by the Liberals in 1847. Meanwhile Bruff and Co. had allegedly charged the interest on these loans to the Stour Valley's accounts.[4]

Protests by Eastern Union shareholders took another form. When the company was first floated, John Cobbold had succeeded in securing a strong body of Yorkshire investors. They now protested at bailing out so obviously unprofitable a concern as the Stour Valley. The 5% on offer was therefore reduced to 3% and the Stour Valley 'persuaded' to forgo its planned extension to Bury. Amidst continuing grumbling the deal was, on this basis, completed. As one Colchester shareholder pointed out, the link with the Stour Valley had proved invaluable in securing their own Parliamentary approval to extend to Stowmarket and Norwich.[5] Indeed, in all these negotiations the only parties to emerge relatively unscathed were those Stour Valley shareholders also involved in the Eastern Union, like, for example, the Hawkins brothers and Peter Bruff who was, of course, engineer to both concerns.

The deal concluded, the Stour Valley was pushed forward to completion. The formal opening to Sudbury was celebrated in July 1849, the guest of honour being the youthful mayor of Colchester, Charles Henry Hawkins, whose timber yards at Sudbury were one of the chief beneficiaries of the new line. Peter Bruff was not there. He was the same day at Burston, seven miles to the south of Norwich, celebrating with all the Eastern Union directors the completion of their line to within striking distance of Norwich in time for the Royal Agricultural Show to be held there that month. High above them waved the banner "Success to the Port of Ipswich". Bruff was however equally proud of his Stour Valley Railway and later made it the subject of a paper before the Institution of Civil Engineers, where his great Chappel viaduct, still in use in 1984, was criticised as an extravagance by that doyen of engineers, Isambard Kingdom Brunel.[6]

The arrival of the Eastern Union line at Norwich brought to a head that larger conflict with the Eastern Counties that many had foreseen. In fact the opening shots had already been fired. In 1848 the Eastern Counties had suddenly demanded a rental of £2,000 from the Eastern Union for the use of their notoriously ill-equipped North Station at

Colchester. The Eastern Union responded by building their own station on the opposite side of the North Station road bridge. They also sought to come to terms with their rivals. Notice was posted of an intention to apply to Parliament to lease or sell the Eastern Union to the Eastern Counties, but that company refused to consider a deal.[7]

The following year, 1849, was dominated by the fall of the railway king, George Hudson, chairman of the Eastern Counties. Dubious practices with the company's finances finally surfaced and he and all his board resigned. Victorian society, which had done so much to foster the glamour that had earlier surrounded him, now rounded on Hudson as a scapegoat, turning his fall into a cautionary tale against the evils of financial greed. Historians have dealt with him more kindly. His practices were not so different from those of his contemporaries; his crime was to offend that Victorian eleventh commandment: thou shalt not be publicly exposed.[8]

Hudson's fall lead to some cautious accommodation between the Eastern Counties and the Eastern Union, including revenue-sharing on London-Colchester-Norwich traffic. This, however, did not last long and threatened litigation by the Eastern Union led by 1851 to open war. The Eastern Counties ran trains to Colchester that were dirty, inconveniently timed and late. Through-bookings were only accepted at rates that denied the Eastern Union any profitable return. Paradoxically, although suffering from a deliberately neglected rail terminal, Colchester merchants saw some advantages in this in their struggle with the port of Ipswich, the chief losers in this railway war. It also postponed for some years the projected Eastern Union rail link to Harwich where Bruff was seeking to build a pier and Hawkins already owned much of the wharfage.[9]

Against this background Colchester learnt of the purchase of the waterworks by Hawkins and Bruff. Negotiations had in fact been under way early in 1850 while Harvey was still trying to rouse the Commissioners into action. Perhaps some Conservative Commissioners knew this. Perhaps this explains the Joint Committee's change of direction in the winter of 1849-50. It is also clear from some surviving letters that Bruff was anxious to complete the purchase before a rival water supply was established by Charrington Nicholl, the East Hill brewer. Nicholl had successfully drilled his own artesian well and possessed the necessary steam power to distribute the water. Indeed, this possibility had already been noted by the Commissioners and urged by Harvey.[10]

All in all it is clear that Bruff had decided that the implication of national legislation, if not of Harvey's Joint Committee, was that before long an increased demand for water was likely in Colchester. But if Bruff had decided that the Waterworks were a good investment, this is not to ignore the degree of entrepreneurial risk involved. It was, in fact, well into 1851 before the tangled legal affairs of the Waterworks

Company were resolved by Bruff's solicitors. Only then was he able to effect a loan and set about some improvements, confiding in a letter to William Hawkins that the company now had a clear income of nearly £700 a year and was "capable of large increase and growth". Appreciating the inadequacy of the Chiswell and Balkerne spring supply, especially since part of the former was now in private ownership and part of the latter accessible to the public, Bruff followed Charrington Nicholl in drilling an artesian well down through the glacial gravel and London clay to the chalk beds below, via which vast quantities of rain water drained to the sea from outcropping boulder clay in Cambridgeshire. Problems however soon followed.[11]

Bruff began by driving 10-inch diameter pipes into the London clay; then he drove pipes of ever decreasing diameter through these earlier pipes. At over 100 feet, in an area of 'green' sand, a 6-inch pipe broke. By using pipes of narrower width than had been sanctioned by Bruff, the bore was continued to 340 feet but the sand seeped in, and the entire well silted up. It was quite useless; they had to start again. The well-borer, Cooper, blamed the pipes, but it was really his fault for using welded sheet-iron pipes instead of cast-iron ones. Three years later he was still arguing the toss with the ironmonger, Catchpool, about payment. Cooper's second bore also failed, so Bruff finally sank a 40-foot well nine feet in diameter and began to bore from here using 8-inch cast-iron pipes. At over 100 feet into the chalk and having no success Copper wanted to stop, but Bruff drove him on for a further 50 feet, thereafter inserting perforated pipes through those already put down. Suddenly the whole hill shook as water broke through and gushed to the surface.[12]

Once more geology had come to Colchester's aid. For during the retreat of the ice shield, glaciers confined to the river valley had exerted great pressure on the chalk beds below. Their departure had caused the land to lift and crack and fissures had appeared in the chalk beds which rapidly filled with water under pressure. The Colchester Waterworks, on the edge of the river valley, lay athwart one of these 'underground reservoirs', and this had now been penetrated by Bruff's bore. For that date it offered an almost limitless supply of water, which one estimate put at 300,000 gallons a day. Indeed, this and a new bore beside it in 1880 proved adequate for all the town's supply until 1906. Installing new engines and boilers and laying additional pipes, Bruff was thus able to greatly augment the town's available supply. Water was now provided for several hours each weekday and, although precise figures are not available, in six years Bruff apparently doubled the weekly output from 450,000 to perhaps 1,000,000 gallons. He was even talking in terms of building a million gallon reservoir.[13]

Bruff's activities at the Waterworks enabled the Commissioners to devote their energies to other concerns, in particular to completing their extensive programme of new main sewers. This was finally achieved in 1854 when the 2,402 feet of 1847 had been extended to 28,080 feet. Harvey took the opportunity provided by the completion of this project to raise again the question of the water supply, and the desirability of adopting the 1848 Act. This would now cost under £200 for the Act and a water rate of sixpence in the pound to secure a general supply. Faced with such an outlay even some of Harvey's friends among the Commissioners balked at the cost and his proposal was rejected in favour of the suggestion of John Taylor, the newspaper proprietor, that stand pipes should be set up to which the poor could have access.[14]

The Commissioners' limited income was, of course, an obstacle to new endeavours. Restricted by their 1847 Act to a maximum two shilling rate, they never asked for less, but were always short of money. Their only other income came from channel dues and, with the continued fall of trade at the Hythe, these fell too. Suggestions that dues should be raised led to comparisons with neighbouring ports and the claim, probably true, that this would merely drive more trade away from Colchester. In fact, the historic linking of maintenance of the Hythe with the improvement of the town was at once a blessing and a curse to the sanitary movement. After 1847 the accounts were technically segregated, and river dues were no longer available to subsidise town improvement, yet the problems of the navigation

The Hythe in 1858 seen from the gasworks. On the far shore stand the timber yards and tar works of the Hawkins brothers, whose wharf was one of the chief beneficiaries of the 1857 compensation agreement. In the foreground a ship has lowered its mast, possibly in deference to Charlie Hawkins, but more probably in order to pass under Hythe Bridge.

continued to absorb both energy and finance. The constant silting of the channel did not stop costly efforts to fight against nature. In 1854-55 the Commissioners exhausted half their limited borrowing powers in a not unsuccessful bid to deepen the channel and eliminate the worst shoals and corners. Unfortunately this also served to modify the main course of the river. More expense followed as the Commissioners consented to partially finance the rebuilding of those wharves left high and dry by these events, particularly when the wharf owners, all leading merchants and members of the Commissioners, threatened litigation. By 1857 one calculation suggested that in ten years the Channel Fund had lost over £10,000 by these exertions. This at least guaranteed the continued membership on the Board of Commissioners of many of the town's leading merchants, but while the improvement of the Hythe channel might be said to increase Colchester's economic prospects, it was harder to demonstrate that an improved water supply would.[15]

It is also noticeable that the Commissioners were more willing to give discussion time to the perennial problem of watering the streets than to watering their inhabitants. The roads of the day had a top surface periodically replenished with small stones which, ground by wheeled vehicles into dust, produced in the dry summer months an unpleasant dust problem. Hence the maintenance by the Commissioners of specially constructed water carts for watering the surface, sometimes twice a day. To this end they negotiated an agreement with Bruff to provide tanks or cisterns conveniently sited in the town to hold the water, much of it perfectly good drinking water, with which to fill the carts. Between 1849 and 1859 the length of public roads watered rose from 2.75 to 6 miles, while the length of roads served by water mains only rose from 3 to 4.5 miles. Yet on any morning during this period fifty to sixty people regularly queued with their buckets at the Hythe, waiting for the sole available public pump to be unlocked.[16]

Thus four more years went by until the passing of the Local Government Act of 1858. This like the Act of 1848 was only permissive, enabling but not compelling bodies like the Commissioners to adopt an Act which included powers to provide a general water supply. This time Harvey prepared the ground more thoroughly. Adopting a Benthamite tactic widely used in the 1840s, he produced and printed his own Report addressed to the Commissioners. Reasoned, factual and unsensational, Harvey's *Report on the Water Supply for Colchester* represents this shrewd man's indictment of Bruff's seven years at the Waterworks. Despite the great increase in water supply that the artesian well had afforded, at most one third of the houses in the town were now supplied. Harvey lists those streets served by the Company's mains. Compared with his 1849 list this shows an increase of only 1.5 miles of roads. Over half of this consisted

JOHN BAWTREE HARVEY in 1883, resplendent in his mayoral robes after 45 years of public service to Colchester. Anxious to quantify his achievements, he kept league tables in his journal of the attendances on the bench of himself and other magistrates. Harvey always comes top.

of Military Road, which had six customers, and the road to North Station which had only three, and which had been completed primarily to effect a lucrative contract with the railway companies. In all, out of 11 miles of continuously inhabited roads within the borough, only 4.5 miles carried water mains. The whole east end of Colchester which, significantly, was both densely populated and contained a high percentage of the poor, had not received an inch of water since 1849.[17]

Indeed, given this very limited extension of the mains, one might question Harvey's suggestion that one third of the town's houses were now supplied. According to Harvey's figures, the weekly output of the waterworks had only doubled. Was it likely, given that water was now supplied on six, not three, days a week, that the number of customers had more than doubled? A more probable proportion of serviced households would be 28-30%. If so, what did the other 70% do?

This Harvey graphically describes. A detailed survey revealed some 450 wells in the town of which barely twelve were truly public. Most of them were disturbingly shallow, invariably contaminated in some way by surface drainage. In addition, the town was regularly plied by water carts which sold water at $\frac{1}{2}$d or 1d a bucket. Some entire families actually made do with two buckets a day, endlessly reusing the same water. This nonetheless cost them £1. 10s. 4d. a year, approximately one third of the annual rent of a small cottage or three times the Waterworks' annual rate for an unrestricted supply to small cottages. Yet this unrestricted supply could mean up to 50 gallons, not two buckets, a day. Why, then, did the Waterworks not have more customers?

Excluding that half of the population who were simply not reached by the water mains, clearly ignorance, if not indolence, played their part in the habits of the poor. More serious however were the hidden costs. Quite apart from the installation charge for pipes from the mains to the kitchen sink, there was the problem of water storage. Harvey pointed out the irony of an intermittent supply, whereby the middle classes spent more money on maintaining water butts and cisterns than on their water rate. Meanwhile, for the poor,

". . . their daily supply, purchased of water carriers, is kept in jugs, dishes or pans which are commonly placed in the single room which serves as kitchen, sitting room and bedroom . . ."

The answer, Harvey concluded, returning to the old theme, was a constant supply available from a tap for 24 hours a day to all sections of the community. Not only had the artesian well sufficient reserves to provide the water, but national calculations had shown that such a universal system could be operated for $2\frac{1}{2}$d per house per week. Finally, Harvey noted that the size of Colchester and the distance of many streets from the present waterworks would require "a reservoir for the supply of the inhabitants at high pressure". In the public debate that followed the publication of Harvey's report, this reservoir became "a tank on top of Balkerne Hill". The idea of Jumbo was born.[18]

4

1860-1870: Mr Bruff Declines

It would be nice to record that Harvey's 1858 *Report* bore immediate fruit. Unfortunately, it did not. True, Harvey himself was, soon afterwards, elected Chairman of the Commissioners, a position he was to hold until his death in 1890. The Commissioners also unanimously adopted the water clauses of the 1848 Act – as the 1858 Act now defined them.[1] But as so often with Victorian legislation, it was one thing to adopt a measure, quite another to make it work. It is now clear that the Commissioners' action produced no result whatsoever in Colchester for at least ten years, and in some respects for longer. The reason lay in an area that Harvey had somewhat skirted round in his report. Essentially a secular sermon, this provided all the necessary argument to justify public action, but it did not cost the exercise in any detail. Yet the Colchester Waterworks was a private company, a monopoly protected by Act of Parliament, whose main aim was to show a return on its capital investment. Bruff was not prepared to extend the mains, unless the additional outlay would be covered by a sufficient number of new customers. For no one, least of all Bruff, claimed that he was making a fortune from the Waterworks.

The problem in part lay in the economic relationship between the poor and the landlords who owned their dwellings. There were, of course, large property owners in Colchester. Often they were the town's leading solicitors who, with their obvious professional advantage, specialised in such investments. However a more typical landlord was a member of the middling classes who had sunk his or her small savings into two or three properties. By carefully controlling overheads, that is to say by neglecting all but essential maintenance, they could secure a larger return in rent than by leaving their money in a bank. The balance however was a delicate one and, at the bottom of the market, was not to be jeopardised by the fixed cost of installing water pipes or the recurring cost of water rates. True, the rent could be raised, but would the tenants pay it? And would the tenant stay?

For at any time in the borough there were always empty houses available for rent and always rooms in lesser properties to be sub-let.[2] Factors like these help to explain why Peter Bruff had by 1858 retreated from his earlier optimism, preferring to give both time and capital to his many other interests, interests which, during this period, put considerable strain upon his cash reserves.

Foremost among these commitments was his position as Engineer and General Manager of the Eastern Union Railway. In 1854 the bitter war with the Eastern Counties finally ended, with the Eastern Union virtually accepting their opponents' terms. "A strong minority of our Board", announced the normally circumspect Cobbold to his opposite number, Waddington, "consider that you have done us". Moreover the terms of the agreement, that the two companies should move towards amalgamation by 1862, left ample room for future manoeuvre. The Eastern Union for example was still expanding, with extensions to Woodbridge and Harwich close to completion. Thus, in the autumn of 1854, when the Engineer of the Eastern Counties suddenly resigned, substance was given to this new accord by an agreement to transfer Bruff from Manager of the Eastern Union to Manager of the Eastern Counties, with continued responsibility for those parts of the Eastern Union, notably the Colchester-Ipswich-Norwich run, which the Eastern Counties was now operating under the agreement.[3]

Bruff had not been in this new position a year when a Board of Trade investigation reported that the Eastern Counties line from London to Norwich via Cambridge was so badly maintained that it was unsafe for the general public. Blame fell on Bruff, the Resident Engineer, and was loudly proclaimed in the columns of *The Railway Times*. Bruff's response was spirited and doubtless justified. He sued *The Railway Times*, and published letters protesting that during his brief period of management all the complaints made by the Board of Trade, particularly about bridges, had been receiving his attention, that speeds had been reduced, and that, in any case, not one accident had occurred. In this he was backed by the Chairman and the Board who, drawing upon proxy votes, fought off demands for a Committee of Enquiry from a majority of the shareholders. In short, Bruff weathered the storms, the confidence of the Chairman and the Board being underlined by a salary increase from £1,000 to £1,500 a year in June 1856. Then, without any public explanation, six months later, Bruff resigned.[4] Why?

It is clear from a letter he wrote shortly before this to his Colchester mentor, William Hawkins, that trouble had arisen between Bruff and the Eastern Counties while he had been ill that autumn. It may have been about payments; it may have been about a clause in Bruff's contract that he should not undertake any new works on his own account. For both matters were soon to become relevant. In any event, Bruff's notice expired in March 1857 and he thereby lost an annual income of £1,500 a year. Indeed for a time he lost more. Bruff's resignation left unresolved the question of various payments, some arising from negotiations he had undertaken on their behalf, some arising over disagreement about the exact nature of his services to the Eastern Counties after the 1854 agreement. This was only resolved before the Court of Queen's Bench in November 1858 when Bruff settled out of court for £1,750 against his own dubious claim of £6,787. Matters did not end here however. Arguments about payment later arose between Bruff and the Eastern Union, and were still being argued in court 16 years later.[5]

Meanwhile, in December 1857, Bruff found himself facing something of a cash crisis. He was, of course, a wealthy man. Only that year in pursuit of his passion for sailing he had commissioned and received the *Silver Star*, a 25-ton schooner, the first iron vessel to be built on the Colne. By his own calculations Bruff was worth at least

RICHARD SANDERSON (1783-1857), City Billbroker and M.P. for Colchester 1832-47, whose contacts proved invaluable in floating railway companies.
"Who is it from London town,
Puffing and sweating did come down,
As tho' afraid to lose his crown?
Poor Richard"
(Liberal poem, 1847)

£40,000, but the bulk of this was tied up in property and shares, whose value might prove more nominal than real.[6] He was also unlucky in the fall of events. In December 1857 Richard Sanderson, city billbroker, died and simultaneously his finance house went into liquidation. Such a demise nicely illustrates that partnership of business and politics which underlay the careers of many backbench Victorian M.P.s. In return for the support of the Hawkins family in securing his re-election as M.P for Colchester, Sanderson had been invaluable in raising loans in the London money market. This, as we have seen, was particularly useful in floating the Stour Valley Railway. Now at the end of 1857 Bruff found himself called upon to meet a £2,000 note from Sanderson's disintegrating partnership. Nor were matters helped by the fact that William Hawkins himself was out of action, housebound and suffering "a severe mental affliction" which had beset him for the past five years. Although he also had become a Colchester M.P., Hawkins had scarcely ever taken his seat, and had been forced to resign earlier that year.

In letters to Sanderson and to his banker, Bruff admitted that the £2,000 could not be paid, but asserted that if the one had been healthy and the other alive "relations between Mr Hawkins and the late Mr Sanderson would have permitted a postponement of payment". His own failure to pay he attributes to

"advances for those abominable Waterworks at Colchester which I had so much trouble to get settled with you for..."[7]

Whether this explanation was strictly true (he did not, for example, sell the *Silver Star*), Bruff's disillusionment with the profitablity of waterworks was more than understandable. For Colchester was not his only undertaking in this direction. In 1857, he was simultaneously encountering difficulty in establishing waterworks at Lowestoft on behalf of Newson Garrett, whose son was married to Bruff's daughter.[8] But more disastrous, if more heroic, had been his activities at Harwich. This ancient port, once host to kings and queens of England arriving and departing for the continent, faced by the mid-19th century little prospect of maintaining its former eminence, if not its raison d'être, without a secure harbour, a railway and an adequate water supply. Bruff was to supply all three, but not without some problems.

In 1851, as consultant engineer, Bruff commenced a long association with the town which, like the best of marriages was to have its difficult moments. First, against considerable opposition from Ipswich, he completed new quays and a pier for the town. Then, in 1854, his Eastern Union Railway finally arrived on a branch line from Manningtree. Water, however, proved the greatest problem.

Hitherto the town had been dependant on rainwater butts and outside sources. When, for example, the port had been put into use during the Napoleonic Wars, water was brought in bulk in barges from Ipswich. Bruff began his search in 1854. As at Colchester he drilled down to the chalk strata, but, contaminated by the adjacent ocean, the water came up salty. At great expense and with equal tenacity, Bruff continued to drill through 700 feet of chalk, putting down expensive cast iron pipes with water-tight joints. Three years later and at 1,100 feet, he hit a hitherto unknown rock, presumed to be a carboniferous limestone. There was no water and the only consequence of this geological revelation, presumably the deepest hole in Essex, was several determined but equally unsuccessful attempts to mine for coal in the area some 45 years later. Harwich had to make do as before with shallow wells and water brought in by Bruff's new railway. And Bruff, who claimed that drilling 60 foot into the unknown rock had cost him a guinea an inch, was "several thousand pounds" out of pocket on the eve of his embarrassment over the Sanderson loan.[9]

In fact Bruff's efforts on behalf of Harwich and its drinking water had only just begun, but this initial failure helps explain why, in 1858, when Harvey persuaded the Colchester Commissioners to adopt the 1848 water clauses, Bruff's public-spiritedness towards the water needs of Colchester was less than evident. Besides, he had other preoccupations. For since 1855 Bruff had been spending money at the seaside spa of Walton-on-the-Naze.

Although it had enjoyed some action in the 18th century, Walton-le-Soken had by 1800 become a coastal backwater, the haunt of smugglers, its unique cliffs not yet subject to fossil hunters. They were, however, subject to coastal erosion. By this means almost all the old village had been engulfed by the sea, including its medieval church, which, although partly in ruins, continued to hold services and weddings until 1796. Thereafter, the roof being considered unsafe, couples were solemnly united in the doorway, pending the building of a new church.[10]

Walton-le-Soken began its gradual transformation into the seaside resort of Walton-on-the-Naze in the first decade of the nineteenth century. In 1806 the mayor of Colchester, William Sparling, organised a picnic party to the beach which proved so popular that it rapidly became a fashionable outing for a number of leading families. Their patronage was soon sought by Edmund Aldridge, a white-haired rustic in blue serge trousers and flannel smock, who improvised the first bathing machine, and set up, almost on the sea's edge, a wooden shack which grew by regular additions as trade increased into the 'Bath Hotel', offering beds at 6d a night, and spray through the open windows at high tide. Unfortunately for Aldridge the waste land he built on was owned by the rectory of All Saints, Colchester, which, to his great grief, finally took possession of this, Walton's first hotel. By this date, however, the same Colchester families had set down new

WILLIAM SPARLING (1766-1816) "eminent solicitor and alderman" of Colchester, whose picnic party, enlivened by local farmers dancing on the beach, first publicised the charms of Walton.

streets, run up houses for summer rental, formed a hotel company, built a real hotel and pier, and instigated an annual regatta.[11]

The modern resort was born, but its commercial potential was constantly and literally undermined by coastal erosion. Appreciating this, a determined effort was made in 1841 to secure adequate sea defences by establishing by Act of Parliament a body of Commissioners with power to raise a local rate. Unfortunately this initiative was defeated almost before it began when, in the struggle that preceded the Bill, the crucial right to tax local landowners was lost. A rating confined to the resort properties, however just, would barely cover the considerable costs of Parliamentary incorporation. The final blow came when the new Commissioners failed to raise a £4,000 loan in the City to finance their improvements. The Commissioners rapidly ceased to meet, no further effort was made to improve the town, and its population and facilities remained little changed for fifteen years.[12]

It may not come as a surprise to learn that one of these unsuccessful Commissioners was William Hawkins, whose father had been an early builder in the town. Hawkins may thus have been responsible for introducing Walton to Peter Bruff. Indeed Bruff's later claim that his association with the resort dated from 1841 could well mean that he had been involved in the establishment of the Commissioners. An equal attraction would have been the regatta. Probably since his Plymouth boyhood Bruff had possessed a passion for the sea and for that sport of rich Victorians, ocean racing. The owner of several expensive yachts and of a house standing on the river Gipping, Bruff was for years the Chairman and driving force behind the Royal Harwich Yacht Club, even visiting the famous New York Yacht Club on their behalf. The 'jetty' at Walton must have early gained his attention, subject as it was during the summer season to regular visits by Ipswich steamers going on to London. Bruff early developed a deep affection for Walton that was long to survive the vicissitudes that accompanied his business ventures there. These began in 1855 when he purchased the Burnt House Farm Estate where the first visitors had lodged nearly 50 years before. He thus acquired, for under £2,000, eighty acres of land and cliffs that lay to the south of the resort and its pier. Walton's 15 years of stagnation were about to end; its combination of picturesque seclusion and relative proximity to the teeming hordes of London was about to be exploited. For Bruff's sharp mind and adventurous temperament had conceived the possibilities not only of developing his new estate, but of establishing a direct rail link with London that would render Walton not significantly harder to reach than Brighton or Margate, two of the fastest growing towns in southern England.[13]

Put in this light, Bruff's resignation from the Eastern Counties may be more readily understood. He was now free to build at Walton (beginning appropriately with an artesian well) and to find backers for the Tendring Hundred Railway, which would run from Colchester via Wivenhoe to Walton. A major bonus was the restoration to comparative health of William Hawkins, who duly became the leading promoter and Chairman of the new company. A more subtle victory, however, was the success of Hawkins, carefully briefed by Bruff, in winning the support of John Cobbold of Ipswich for the scheme. Not only was the old Eastern Union partnership thereby reunited, but the potential rival interests of Ipswich were hopefully neutralised. In the event the Tendring Hundred line took so long to arrive at Wivenhoe that a rival scheme was mounted, to which Cobbold lent his name and capital, for taking a railway from Ipswich via Mistley to Walton. In fact the Mistley-Walton line was never completed, but

The only surviving likeness of WILLIAM WARWICK HAWKINS M.P. leaves many questions unanswered about the iron-willed man who left so firm a mark on mid-Victorian Colchester, yet suffered for several years "a severe mental affliction".

nothing was more calculated to stimulate interested parties in Colchester and silence any misgivings about Bruff's role in the matter than the prospect of losing to the old enemy, Ipswich, both the agricultural trade of the Tendring Hundred and a rail link with a second Brighton.[14]

Not least among the factors commending the new railway to Colchester was that the first stage was to run to Wivenhoe. For the efforts of the Commissioners to render the tidal Colne suitable for large shipping had inevitably failed. The bulk of the coal arriving by sea still travelled at some expense by lighters from Wivenhoe to the Hythe. The cost-reducing benefits of a railway were therefore an important argument made at the Parliamentary Enquiry, and one which the Commissioners fully supported. All of this sheds interesting light on the £60,000 ship canal once proposed by Hawkins and Bruff. The same gentlemen were now offering similar benefits from a £15,000 railway. Their other project, the Hythe rail loop, also took on new significance, since the starting point for the Wivenhoe railway was to be a new station at the Hythe. The Hythe loop, operated under a 999 year lease by the Eastern Union Railway, would therefore provide the only access for the Eastern Counties Railway when (and if) it brought thousands of travellers from London to the new East Coast resorts. Of course the Eastern Union and the Eastern Counties were committed to amalgamation by 1862, but in 1859, when the Tendring Hundred proposal came before Parliament, not only did some of the Eastern Union directors still wonder whether amalgamation would ever happen, but all of them were anxious to salvage the best financial bargain from the arrangement. Thus should the amalgamation face eleventh hour problems, or should some leverage be required, access over the Hythe loop might prove significant: for the Eastern Union of which Cobbold was Chairman, Hawkins a Director and Bruff the late Engineer, and the Tendring Hundred of which Bruff, Hawkins and Cobbold were promoters looked suspiciously like the same people. This fact was not missed at the Parliamentary Enquiry. But when asked why he had not suggested the Tendring Railway while Engineer and General Manager to the Eastern Counties, Bruff, whose engineering initiatives had been legion, blandly answered that they hadn't asked him. In any case, he asserted, it was no part of a mere engineer's job to prompt his employers' actions. One hopes he kept a straight face when saying this.[15]

There is a final twist to this marriage of public good and private interest. The terminus of the new railway was not to be the Hythe, but a new station constructed far closer to the town centre at St Botolph's Corner, where the Hawkins brothers had large timber yards, and where St Botolph's House, the Hawkins's home, became the Board Room of the new company. The rail approach to St Botolph's was up that same valley down which the town's main sewer ran in the opposite direction. The route that Bruff followed first threatened to destroy the Childwell Alley Spring, then left it on the far side of a steep footbridge, cut off from its main customers, the inhabitants of Magdalen Street. Only protests by the Commissioners to Bruff and an outlay of £50 on their part, re-established a well-head on the near side of the line.[16]

The progress of the Tendring Hundred Railway was painfully slow. Despite the near absence of engineering difficulties, it took four years to reach Wivenhoe, eight years to reach Walton, plagued by shortage of finance, Parliamentary expenses and endless delays. The worst blow came in 1866 with the bankruptcy of the contractor, Monroe, himself a major shareholder. The Company had no choice but to raise more capital and complete the line themselves under Bruff's personal direction. The Tendring Hundred finally opened to Walton in 1867, £20,000 in debt. For one man it was truly the end of the line. William Warwick Hawkins lost heavily on the project. He lived only nine months longer. The strong man of Colchester for 25 years was not strong in body. He died at the early age of 52 from the dropsy brought on by his weak heart. "A more open-handed and kind-hearted man never lived", declared a leading Conservative.[17]

Bruff's Walton seen from the sea in 1871, showing Bruff's pier, Bruff's breakwaters, Bruff's sea wall, Bruff's Crescent and Bruff's Clifton Hotel complex.

The railway reached a Walton much changed since Bruff's arrival 12 years before. Between 1858 and 1862 he had built sea defences and concrete walks to protect his newly acquired estate, put down an artesian well, installed steam engines to pump water to the whole town, established gas works and street lighting, laid out two crescents of houses, built the town's largest hotel, the Clifton, with its associated Baths and Assembly Rooms and, in 1863, secured Parliamentary powers to build a second and larger pier to service this new development. Indeed such was Bruff's dominance of Walton, that a future opponent was to remonstrate

> "that Mr Bruff seemed to be the landowner, the Water Company, the Pier Company and the Commissioners"

"At least", responded Bruff's counsel, conscious of his client's racy humour, "he is not the vicar as well". For the moment however public misgivings about Bruff's monopoly status lay in the future. The concern in 1864 was the continued non-arrival of the railway. Bruff made this his excuse for delaying the start of Walton's second pier, though a more likely explanation was a shortage of capital. For in 1864 Bruff was at last able to purchase a large stretch of deserted coastline near the village of Clacton and the entire hamlet of Frinton: total population sixteen. The subsequent development of both these resorts was to be initiated by Bruff, and within a year of their purchase he made clear his intentions. Official notices were published of plans to build a branch line to within 60 yards of the deserted cliffs at Clacton, with a 300 yard pier opposite the point of its arrival. [18]

Notwithstanding these coastal preoccupations, Bruff found time the following year to switch his attention from Walton to Harwich, once more to renew his efforts to provide that town with an adequate water supply. Steam pumps were installed to bring water from a new bore at Dovercourt, an operation which he later admitted yielded less than 1% return on his outlay. In the process however he was also appointed Engineer to the Conservancy Board then being set up to save Harwich harbour. For the coastal erosion that was rendering sea defences at Walton so ruinously expensive to maintain presented Harwich with the converse problem. Septaria stone, used in making Roman cement, had been dredged from the coast at Felixstowe in such large quantities that a natural underwater breakwater had been removed. As a result the sandy cliffs were eaten into and their contents swept south in such volumes that a sand and shingle bar seemed likely to block the entrance to the Stour and Orwell estuaries, thereby threatening the future of both Ipswich and Harwich as ports. Some £130,000 had already been spent by the Admiralty when Bruff, acting on an earlier survey, constructed a curved jetty at Landguard Point which swiftly destroyed the bar and shortened the Point. Ipswich and Harwich were saved and the future development of Parkeston Quay, if not Felixstowe Docks, was secured. Viewed from the 1980s this might be considered Bruff's greatest achievement of all. [19]

With such diverse commitments throughout the Eastern Counties, one might well wonder what time this left for the affairs of the Colchester Waterworks. The answer would be, not a lot. The only important extension to its activities involved the Army.

Absent since the Napoleonic Wars, the Army had returned to Colchester in 1855 as a permanent peacetime garrison, greatly boosting the economy of the town. It had also exacerbated health problems. Quite apart from an increase in venereal disease, for which a specialist hospital was built, and the compulsory examination of prostitutes which followed, there was the question of Army sewage. This all discharged via that main sewer running from St Botolph's Corner to the the river and came dangerously close to exceeding its capacity, particularly in its lower reaches which were still an open ditch.

In 1862 the extensive infantry garrison was joined by cavalry barracks. Water was now a pressing need, for it is a nice comment on Victorian realities that horses, those fundamental units of urban transport, required more water than human beings. Thus one 1860 encyclopaedia estimated that while every adult needed a gallon a day for drinking, washing and cleaning, every horse drank eight to twelve gallons, and needed three to four gallons for grooming. Consequently, when a large artesian bore drilled on Army land beside Butt Road failed to provide any water, the situation was serious. The only alternative was to enter into a separate contract with Bruff to meet their urgent need.[20]

Thus did Peter Bruff occupy the 1860s. And throughout these busy years, he steadily stonewalled all efforts by the Commissioners to persuade him to extend the mains of the Colchester Waterworks. His obvious preoccupation elsewhere even led Harvey to propose that the Commissioners should purchase the Waterworks for the town. A month's negotiations followed, but the two parties were so far apart in agreeing a price that the suggestion was finally dropped. The Commissioners resorted instead to trying to persuade Bruff to supply 'cottage' properties at a sufficiently low rate to justify the Commissioners in compelling landlords to install mains water under the 1858 Local Government Act. Their steady persistence led Bruff to remonstrate:

> "There have been so many negotiations between the Commissioners and the Company which have led to no practical result, and as I apprehend the Local Government Act will not be adopted without arrangements for a constant service, and the Commissioners requirements . . . being entirely supplied by the Company, it appears to me individually that it would be useless and impracticable to further negotiate . . ."[21]

True, Bruff subsequently agreed to supply cottages at twopence a week, but even the Commissioners' willingness to compel landlords to install service pipes did not persuade him to extend his mains down Magdalen Street to the Hythe, and this despite a report in the *Essex Standard* of March 1866 that he was about to do so. Monroe's bankruptcy in April doubtless explains why he did not. In the end the miller, Edward Marriage, personally met the cost of drilling an artesian well at the Hythe to offset the shortage there.

Bruff and the Commissioners had in fact reached a state of impasse. The essential dilemma was summed up by Bruff in 1869:

> "If the Commissioners will take £20 of water a year at the Hythe, we will carry it there . . ."

To this the Commissioners' considered reply was:

> "We cannot offer the Waterworks Company any guarantee on behalf of private consumers".[22]

Of course such unhurried discussion was not unaffected by the fact that Colchester was widely considered to be a healthy town, with an overall death rate below the national average. More significantly, it had not been visited by the last national epidemic of cholera in 1866. Figures published at the height of the outbreak nicely illustrate this, if we compare Colchester with Romford, an Essex town of comparable size, and West Ham, by now an extension of the East End of London.

Town	Approx. Population	Death from Cholera	Death from Diarrhoea
Colchester	24,000	0	2
Romford	26,000	9	12
West Ham	59,000	58	380

The only warning comment in the Registrar General's otherwise complacent report on Colchester was that 'fever' could invariably be found round the river into which the town's sewage all flowed.

Thus it was that by 1870, twelve years after Harvey's pamphlet had been published, the water supply of Colchester had not been significantly extended, while the town's population had risen by over 3,000. The only real mains extension had been along Lexden Road, now developing as a select middle class housing area. This extension was only made possible by placing a large storage tank, paid for by the Commissioners, at one end of Lexden Road. The tank was constructed by a new and energetic engineering firm, recently established in the town, and it represented, though perhaps he did not realise it, the first involvement of its founder, James Paxman, with the 'Colchester water question'. It was not to be his last.[23]

Cavalry Barracks, Colchester

5

1870-1878: Seasides and Gasworks

Paxman's new engineering works symbolised an important change that was coming over the economy of Colchester as the 1870s progressed. A town hitherto dependant on agriculture, and to a lesser extent the Army, was developing a significant industrial base. Engineering, boot and shoe making, clothing factories and the building trades were, by the 1880s, to add substantially to the town's prosperity. There was also during the 1870s a considerable expansion of the housing stock, brick-built, slate-roofed and a great improvement on existing properties. Every prospect existed that this new housing might, from the outset, be plumbed for mains water, if not installed with water closets. This was particularly relevant at the east end of the town, hitherto so neglected, as the first stages unfolded of what was subsequently labelled the 'New Town' area, extending in an arc between Military Road and Magdalen Street.[1]

Such developments may well have been a factor in Bruff's more energetic approach to the Waterworks in this decade. There was now a greater prospect of it becoming a profitable exercise. Equally relevant was the decline of his railway activities. The great days of railway speculation were long since past and many of the branch lines Bruff had constructed for the Eastern Union were running at a loss. Nowhere was this more true than with his latest undertaking, the Tendring Hundred Railway, hopelessly in debt and paying not a farthing dividend. Its completion had only been made possible by financial assistance from the Great Eastern Railway (G.E.R.) the title of the company formed from the long anticipated amalgamation of the Eastern Union and the Eastern Counties. However, bailing out the Tendring Hundred and other equally unprofitable branch lines almost proved to be the straw that broke the camel's back. In 1867 the G.E.R., which now represented almost the entire railway network of East

Anglia, was placed in the hands of receivers, and was only dragged back from the brink by the appointment of a new Chairman. Having acquired over two decades an unenviable record for dubious practices, the company now secured a Chairman of unimpeachable rectitude in Lord Cranborne, soon to become the Marquis of Salisbury, a future Prime Minister of England. Salisbury was insistent that branch lines under G.E.R. control should get no traffic receipts until their debts to the parent company were paid, and this, since the death of William Hawkins, the Tendring Hundred seemed unlikely to do. Gone were the plans that Bruff had fostered of an extension of the line to Walton Channel and the construction there of a wharf for the accommodation of steam boats, free from the ravages of coastal erosion.[2]

Indeed by 1868 Bruff was undoubtedly reconsidering the wisdom of unilateral developments at Walton. Although the terminus of the new railway was sited, not surprisingly, beside his own developments to the south of the town, it is clear that overall Bruff was involved in much expense in his Walton undertakings. The continued fight against the erosion of the cliffs remained a losing battle, one of the sufferers being Bruff's own Clifton Hotel complex. Indeed, eventually, even the Burnt House Farm was to succumb to the sea.[3]

Consequently, one of Bruff's first moves, following the arrival of the railway, was to resuscitate the moribund Improvement Commissioners, successfully assembling at the Clifton Hotel their first quorate meeting for 26 years. A more collective approach to the development of the resort was clearly necessary if he were to realise the ambitious plans he still fostered of securing the coastal defences, and running a tramway along the cliffs to Frinton, 400 acres of which he already owned. By becoming himself a leading Commissioner, Bruff faced one of those irritating conflicts of interest so abhorrent to John Taylor of Colchester: Bruff also owned the Walton Gas and Waterworks. He therefore deemed it prudent to convert these into a limited liability company in order to do business with the Commissioners, leaving for the future the awkward consideration of whether the Commissioners would be happy with its products.[4]

Bruff's experience at Walton doubtless influenced his policy towards his undeveloped acres at Clacton. Initially, of course, the débâcle of the Tendring Hundred Railway destroyed any hope of proceeding with the Thorpe and Clacton line which had received Parliamentary approval in 1866. A warrant for its abandonment was even issued in 1872. One problem was that a number of local landowners, who were reluctant to see a major seaside resort develop, made difficulties about selling the required land, but the real obstacle at this stage was the G.E.R., which under its new Chairman was unwilling to underwrite so speculative a venture.

Frustrated in his attempt to bring customers to Clacton by rail, Bruff turned naturally to the sea. Indeed this important highway had always been part of his plans. His 1866 Railway Bill had included provision for a 300 yard pier, a structure sufficiently extensive to facilitate the unloading of passengers at most states of the tide. A number of rival companies now operated steamboats in the Thames and there was keen competition for the 'day excursion' trade. The Woolwich Steam Packet Company for example ran as far as Ipswich, regularly stopping at Walton and Harwich on the way. Bruff now succeeded in interesting its chairman, William Parry Jackson, in the possibilities of a new resort at Clacton. At a celebrated meeting on the deserted beach in 1870 the two men strode the sands, discussing the lay-out and no doubt the funding of a new seaside resort.[5]

The deal appears to have included an undertaking by the Woolwich Company to patronise Bruff's other resort area at Walton. For in the winter that followed Bruff completed the long postponed Clifton pier which, reaching out like an arm from the Clifton Hotel to greet new customers, left little doubt as to its true purpose. A press release justified its construction on the grounds that its length would permit the Woolwich steamers to berth at all tides, a claim which was treated with derision by long-standing residents. Not only did the 1830 'jetty' stand in far deeper water, but, close to the heart of older Walton, it offered far better access for carriages than the rugged road from the Clifton Hotel. The new pier thus marked an important moment in a growing public reassessment of Bruff's relationship to the resort.[6]

Meanwhile, in 1871, appropriately the year in which the Bank Holiday Act was passed, Clacton-on-Sea was launched. The image is not inappropriate; Clacton was marketed in a distinctly modern manner. Bruff took shares in the Woolwich Company and a much shorter pier was hastily constructed in time for the summer season. On a hot Thursday in July an estimated 700 to 800 people, some from as far as Colchester, assembled on Clacton beach to witness the arrival of the large steamer, *Albert Edward*, which had set out from Woolwich that morning with 200 invited guests of the Woolwich Company. Most of the Directors were also present to be escorted onto the pier head by Peter Bruff himself. Since the resort did not boast a single public building, one is bound to wonder at the catering and personal facilities that such a multitude would require. There was also the troublesome attention they received from flies which swarmed in from the bean fields on top of the cliffs. In the event the state of the tide kept the visit to little more than an hour, during which "curious rustics" were invited on board the *Albert Edward*. This elaborate promotional exercise was glowingly and extensively reported in the Kent and London press, an operation much facilitated by W.P. Jackson's ownership of two newspapers.[7]

The next year building began on Bruff's land to the west of the pier, following a symmetrical plan drawn up by Bruff and centred on the pier. More significant however was the simultaneous establishment of the Clacton-on-Sea Hotel Company Ltd., the first of some eight Clacton development companies floated during the next ten years which drew predominantly on Woolwich and London capital. Indeed several were not even advertised in the Colchester press. These companies represented the systematic development of Clacton-on-Sea as a business venture, based initially on the resources of the Woolwich Steam Packet Company, who saw in the new resort a potential rival to Margate over which they might have monopoly control. In this they were not entirely at one with Peter Bruff. He had envisaged a more limited high class development which, confined to the land he owned, would from the outset maintain a high standard of public utilities. As one of Jackson's fulsome press reports put it:

"... being an entirely new creation, and not the adaptation of an existing town, none of the evils inseparable from the old watering places will be allowed to exist in it. There will be no slums, nor any object that can offend the eye".[8]

This aim was behind Bruff's 'Deed of Mutual Covenant', acceptance of which was obligatory on all those who bought plots of land from him during the early stages of development. It committed owners or occupiers to a special rate payable to Bruff for the maintenance of drainage, paving, lighting and improvement. He thus became in effect

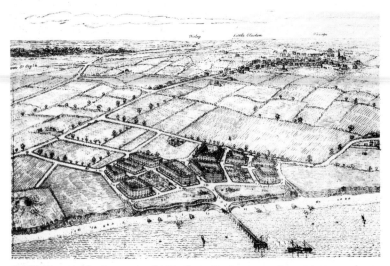

Bruff's Clacton: a bird's eye view of 1871 shows the planned symmetrical lay-out of the new resort, only the eastern half of which was subsequently adopted. In the distance lies the village of Great Clacton.

a one-man Improvement Commission, thereby avoiding the necessity for that body of gentlemen who at Walton had hitherto proved so ineffectual. But if Bruff aspired to build Clacton on a sound basis, avoiding the drawbacks that limited resources had imposed on Walton for 50 years, direction was increasingly beyond his control. Outside capital was calling the tune, as the string of 'Woolwich' companies was spawned. Although Bruff bought yet more land in 1876, a new parent company, the Clacton-on-Sea Land, Building and Investment Company, registered in 1877, came to dominate the resort, buying up all Bruff's original acres for £9,000 and his Deed of Covenant for £2,000, plus £4,000 for money owed to him under this scheme. Bruff had done very well out of Clacton financially, but he was no more the father of the resort. Indeed, even a promise made to Bruff to develop the land west of the pier in line with his symmetrical plan was not observed. More extensive building, the arrival of the railway in 1882 and a massive increase in the number of steam boat passengers began to tilt the delicate balance away from a select resort of substantial properties to a seaside town catering for day trippers and London excursionists. An exclusive and high class resort was to be developed instead at Frinton during the following decades on land already owned by Bruff.

Thus it was that by the mid-1870s Bruff was no longer involved in major railway undertakings, while his direct control over events at Walton and Clacton was less than it had earlier been. Despite being also involved in developing sewerage systems for Ipswich and Lowestoft, one gets the impression that during these years the Colchester Waterworks occasionally received his full attention.[9]

Significantly Bruff's first move at Colchester was to increase his sources of supply. This is interesting in view of the apparently limitless capacity that was claimed for his artesian well at the Balkerne Works. The additional supplies came from the ancient springs. First the Sheepen Spring, whose well-head still stands close to the end of Sheepen Road, was piped to the Balkerne Works. Next Bruff purchased from his own Tendring Hundred Railway the remains of the Childwell Alley Spring that had been breached by the railway cutting. Finally, he concluded a lease for the old St Botolph's Brewery spring which, stored in a small watertower, and pumped by a Paxman engine, could serve the Magdalen Street area. For Bruff's chief concern in taking over the last two sources was the difficulty of reaching the east end of Colchester from the existing Balkerne Works.

There were of course those among the Commissioners who argued that a service for the whole borough could more effectively be achieved by a water-tower on top of Balkerne Hill. Indeed by 1866 plans had been drawn up and the tower costed at £3,000. Bruff was not convinced; besides, he had other priorities: at long last the area of the town served by his mains had begun to grow. Pipes were laid down

East Hill as far as Greenstead Road and down Magdalen Street to the Hythe; while the coming of the Essex Agricultural Show to Lexden Park in 1876 was made the occasion to run mains water a further mile down Lexden Road.[10] In short, Bruff could increasingly claim, if necessary in a court of law, that he now served all the built-up area of Colchester, and that he was the first person actually to fulfil the obligations undertaken in so cavalier a style by Ralph Dodd's Act of Parliament, the Act by which Bruff still claimed sole right to provide a public water supply to the town. Was there any need for this? In truth there was.

Matters had been transformed by the passing of the Public Health Acts of 1872 and 1875. Together they represented a revolution in local government for Colchester. The one transferred all matters relating to public health from the Commissioners to the Borough Council, the other gave wide powers of raising loans and firmly placed upon the Council the obligation of providing a satisfactory water supply. This might be achieved either by municipally initiated works or by an existing private company. Indeed such was the contemporary regard for existing property rights that municipalities were not permitted to construct their own works where a statutory company was satisfactorily providing a town's needs and meeting the terms laid down in its Act of Incorporation. After 1875, it was legitimate to ask whether Peter Bruff's company was.

A third possibility existed, which by 1875 had already been adopted by 127 local authorities, most notably by Birmingham, which under the leadership of Joseph Chamberlain, Lord Salisbury's future Cabinet colleague, was rapidly becoming Britain's most dynamic urban centre. Chamberlain championed 'gas and water socialism': the purchase of these two basic utilities by a town, to be operated as a public service, and, it was claimed, as a profitable undertaking for the benefit of the ratepayers.[11]

It is interesting to trace the process by which this seemingly revolutionary ideology came to be all but universally accepted in Colchester with regard to Bruff's waterworks, both by the legal and commercial gentlemen who made up the Borough Council, as well as by the articulate middle classes who represented public opinion in the town. But to understand water, we must first consider gas.

Colchester Gasworks were the first to be built in Essex and at a very early date, even by national standards. Established in Duck Lane (now Northgate Street) in 1817, within two years the whole High Street was lit by public lamps. So early an undertaking had its problems. Costs were high and some initial experiments quite literally misfired. Nevertheless, by 1826 the Colchester Gaslight and Coke Company had a share capital of £10,000, and in 1838 made an important decision to increase its capital and build new works at the Hythe, where that essential raw material, coal, could be unloaded direct from barges.

These new works were now leased to a series of working partners, few of whom grew rich in the process. Nor was any decision made to secure their monopoly by an Act of Parliament. Matters reached a head in 1847 when John Theobald and Jabez Church (the latter an experienced gas engineer), facing bankruptcy, surrendered their lease to Thomas Joslin, a Cheltenham chemist whose cousin, George Joslin, was a leading Colchester ironmonger. Joslin got into all sorts of trouble, and with speculation rising that the forthcoming Public Health Act might place gas and water supply under the control of local authorities, a public agitation organised by Bawtree Harvey brought pressure on the Gas Company to considerably reduce their prices. Such success was an important factor in Harvey's election to the Commissioners the following year but was the last straw for Thomas Joslin. Early in 1849 he fled the town, leaving his sureties, George Joslin and Daniel Mills to salvage his debts.[12]

This they did tolerably well. Under the management of George Joslin's son, also George, they gradually brought the enterprise into a state of profit. In this they were much aided by their own monopoly position, by an expanding demand for the product, and by a policy which neglected capital investment and technical improvements while yet charging high prices. Protests from the Commissioners regularly occurred, followed by the sort of protracted but unproductive negotiations we have already seen taking place with Bruff over the Waterworks.

Part of the trouble was that Joslin and Mills were merely the lessees of the Colchester Gaslight and Coke Company, paying, in effect, a fixed rental to a Board of Directors who in turn declared a set dividend to their shareholders. This Board included a number of leading citizens who were not only merchants in their own right but, in some cases, elected members of the Commissioners. Such a conflict of interests was no more remarkable than the reservation of seats among the Commissioners for large ship owners, the urging by the Hawkins brothers of a wet dock leading to their own private quays, or the special pleadings of the coal-merchant, Thomas Moy, for a reduction in the port dues on coal. Few of the town's businessmen could serve as Commissioners without their business interests being, sooner or later, influenced by the Commissioners' decisions. This however need not prevent a corporate pursuit of what was perceived as the public good. The subsequent history of the Commissioners' relations with the Gas Company sheds interesting light on this dilemma.

In 1865 John Bawtree Harvey and his close political ally, Thomas Catchpool, were invited to join the Board of the Gas Company. Both were Commissioners; both were stout campaigners for the public good. In a decision doubtless linked with these two men's arrival, the Gas Company terminated their lease to Joslin and Mills, appointed a professional gas manager, and undertook the production of gas themselves, hoping thereby to provide a better service to the town. Hardly had this decision been taken, when a group of Colchester citizens calling themselves the Gas Consumers Company advertised in the Colchester press their intention of securing an Act of Parliament to grant them power to supply gas to the town. Faced with the ruinous competition that this represented, the Gas Company had no alternative but to do likewise with an Act of their own.[13] It is not clear who the main proponents of the Gas Consumers Company were, but a key figure was Frederick Blomfield Philbrick.

A prominent local solicitor, Fred Philbrick was also a member of the Borough Council and a leading Liberal. Indeed, as a young man, when the Liberals had briefly ruled Colchester, he had been Town Clerk, until, that is, the Conservatives took over. Thereafter his capacity to take umbrage had led him to part company with the local party and offer his services to Harwich instead, where he had successively become Town Clerk, Liberal Party Agent and Clerk to Bruff's Conservation Board. Philbrick had three sons, the second of whom, Horace, following in his father's footsteps, became both a solicitor and Liberal Party Agent at Colchester. It was Horace Philbrick who acted as solicitor to the Gas Consumers Company, while his father provided the land at the Hythe on which the proposed new gasworks would be built.[14]

A crucial role was now taken by Bawtree Harvey. Faced with the challenge of the Gas Consumers and the need to steer a rival Bill of Incorporation through Parliament, Harvey rapidly moved to the chair of the Gas Company. Previous chairmen had been long-standing members and majority shareholders. Harvey was neither. Some might consider this a classic case of gamekeeper turned poacher. Harvey perceived it as a service to the community.

By employing experienced Parliamentary advisers, Harvey soon established that the Gas Consumers had offended some technicalities in submitting their Bill to Parliament. Increasingly it emerged that the Gas Consumers had little following in the town and, more significantly, among the ranks of the Commissioners. Large costs threatened them, and, in their hour of need, they came to talk to Harvey. At a crucial meeting between Harvey, Catchpool, Philbrick and Barnes, all leading Liberals in the town, terms were agreed whereby the Gas Consumers would withdraw their Bill and give their support to the Gas Company's Bill in return for having their existing costs met. This however was to reckon without the Commissioners. Were they not the guardians of the public good as well as (via the public lamps) the Gas Company's best customer?[15]

The Commissioners therefore established a Committee - which included Thomas Catchpool - to treat with the Gas Company over their new Bill. This, they noted, would permit charges of 4/6d per 1000 cubic feet of gas, when the current rate at Ipswich was 3/9d and at Norwich 3/6d. The clauses governing purity were also distinctly vague. The Committee therefore insisted that the maximum price should be 4/3d, that specific details for testing purity should be written into the new Act, and that the charge for public lamps should be one eighth less than that for private consumers. Knowing the likely cost of a contested Bill, the Gas Company felt bound to meet these demands, but negotiations went on to the last minute, with the Company meeting in Harvey's own house and Catchpool acting as go-between. Even so there was a hiccup when the Bill came before the House of Lords, occasioning more expense and delay. The Commissioners might well feel they had won a good bargain for the town. Writing of these events years later Harvey bitterly recalled:

"The cost to the Company of this Act was £1167..3s.2d. . . . This enormous expense of an unopposed Bill was occasioned by the abortive 'Gas Consumers Bill', and the protracted efforts of the Town Commissioners to intro-duce clauses into the Bill which, if admitted, would have seriously impaired the interests of the Company, without any advantage whatever to the public".[16]

Were these comments justifiable? Certainly the Commissioners' action was to have long-term consequences.

There is also great irony in these events coming, as they did, at the very moment when Monroe, contractor to the Tendring Hundred Railway, was going bankrupt and Peter Bruff was demonstrating how much a public water supply for the poor depended on his whim or his liquidity. Yet throughout the public debate surrounding the 'gas question' in 1866 there was no suggestion that the Commissioners, the relevant body at this stage, should bid themselves for public ownership of the Company, then capitalised, or rather overcapitalised, at £20,000. In reality, with their borrowing power restricted to £10,000, and most of this already drawn, they could not have done so. Harvey and some five fellow Commissioners who were also Gas Company shareholders took the pragmatic view, arguing that under their management the public would be better served by an improved supply and a more efficiently run body.

Controversy rather arose over the right of these six gentlemen to continue as Commissioners, a body which, with its responsibility for public lighting was virtually the Gas Company's best customer. An anonymous letter appeared in the *Essex Standard,* denouncing the gang of six on the grounds that, since the Gas Company had terminated its lease to Joslin and Mills and was producing its own gas, the six shareholders were financially benefitting from the contract with the Commissioners of which they were also members. Although not mentioned by name, no one was more implicated than John Bawtree Harvey, now both Chairman of the Commissioners and Chairman of the Gas Company.

Now there was nothing unusual in Victorian Colchester about rude or anonymous letters to the press, but on this occasion there was an uproar, which cannot solely be explained in terms of one offensive phrase that was rapidly deleted from the second edition of the paper. The extraordinary intensity of the passions released illustrates how sensitive public men had become to that fine dividing line between public good and private profit and, in a close community like Colchester, the charge of civic irregularity. The Commisioners, if not the Borough Council, prided themselves upon their lack of jobbery.[17]

The letter had a significant first effect. When the Commissioners' monthly meeting took place three days later, only two turned up. The meeting had to be abandoned, an almost unprecedented happening. Clearly some checking up was going on. The next month, fortified no doubt with legal reassurances, the Commissioners assembled in force to vent their anger with extraordinary unanimity on their fellow Commissioner, John Taylor of the *Essex Standard*, who had published

the offending letter. One by one they demanded that he should reveal the name of the writer, an action he had already refused to take in correspondence in his paper. It is of course possible that they believed that Taylor wrote the letter himself, except that this was specifically denied by more than one speaker. Such hostility was the more remarkable given the outspoken stand John Taylor had frequently taken over matters affecting the public interest. He more than anyone had pointed out the private benefits of Bruff's ship canal in 1847.

Nor did the legal nicety on which the six Commissioners took their stand carry more than technical weight. Protection was provided by the fact that since the Commissioners' contract with Joslin and Mills was an annual one which lasted until

JOHN TAYLOR, owner of the Essex Standard, midwife of the Colchester Museum and the Colchester Co-op, champion of public libraries, public footpaths and public accountability, died a disappointed man.

midsummer, the Gas Company had arranged for Joslin and Mills to meet the cost of the gas actually being provided by the Gas Company to itself until that date. The Commissioners were therefore still contracted with Joslin and Mills and the six were not ultra vires. With this defence they rounded on Taylor. Even John Bawtree Harvey, whose tact and ability to leave things unsaid was often paraded as his crowning asset, added his own rebuke. Had he been in Taylor's position, he claimed, rather than rush so readily to judgement, he would have closely examined the legal situation to establish by what means six such valuable public servants might retain their seats as Commissioners. Clearly this is exactly what John Bawtree Harvey himself had done.

The bitterness engendered by this incident certainly took its toll. Protesting at the painful position he found himself in, Thomas Catchpool abstained from several meetings of the Commissioners. John Taylor's response was more dramatic. Despite efforts on all sides to dissuade him, he resigned his seat. The same year he also sold the *Essex Standard* which he had owned and edited for 35 years, announcing his intention of leaving the town in which he had lived his entire life. He was not gone two months when, suddenly, he died. In his last letter, published posthumously, he described himself as "a townsman who under circumstances of some trial was retiring from a long public life". He was just 59.[18]

Meanwhile, relations between the Commissioners and the newly incorporated Gas Company remained cool. In 1871 growing complaints about the quality of gas led to rival reports, both by qualified gas engineers, commissioned first by the Commissioners and then by the Gas Company. In practice both reports revealed a disturbingly high ammonia content in the gas, but disagreement continued over the level of brightness that the Company were under an obligation to supply. Once more the strains of a divided loyalty brought Catchpool to the brink of resignation from the Commissioners, a gesture which Harvey dissuaded him from making. All this makes Harvey's own performance the more remarkable. Through seven months of disagreement he continued to act as chairman to both bodies, only once standing down as Chairman of the Commissioners in order to argue the Gas Company's case. Stern words were exchanged and the Gas Company to an extent gave way, but at the end Harvey was still accorded by his opponents the expressions of praise for his tact and his diplomacy that were rapidly becoming automatic. This was just as well, for the financial restrictions with which the Commissioners had circumscribed the Gas Company were about to reach a crisis.[19]

By 1872-73 the demand for British coal had risen at such a rate that the so-called 'coal famine' hit the nation. Coal prices doubled. This and increased labour costs compelled the Gas Company to pay reduced dividends to its shareholders in 1873 and no dividends at all in 1874.

Already charging their maximum of 4/3d per 1000 cubic feet and believing that their economic difficulties would prevent them raising fresh capital, the Gas Company saw no way of replacing their deteriorating plant or of increasing their output to meet a steadily expanding demand. The only solution was a new Act of Parliament to secure a rise in the minimum price to 5/6d and an end to the one eighth reduction for the supply of public lamps, an operation which was now running at a net loss to the Gas Company.

By this date, of course, public lamps were the concern of the Town Council, not the Commissioners, though many of the personnel were just the same. Besides, the matter of the Gas Company's Amended Bill soon became the concern of the wider community. The Council's attitude was from the first

HENRY JONES spoiling for a fight with the Gas Company, the Borough Police, the Liberal Party or, as on one dark night in 1857, a duty sergeant at the Infantry Barracks.

suspicious, and when they received the opinion of a special sub-committee, downright hostile. They resolved to formally oppose the Bill in Parliament.

This same view was then carried at a Public Meeting in the town with only two real dissentients, both Liberal friends of Harvey. That might be significant, for the chief promoters of the case against the Gas Bill were all connected with the active Conservative leadership of Colchester. Firstly there was Charles Henry Hawkins, the surviving Hawkins brother. Then there was the Town Clerk, Sayers Turner, Hawkins's political confidant, for long regarded by the Liberals as "wire puller in chief" in the political affairs of the borough. Thirdly there was the aging Fred Philbrick, a Liberal it is true, but with a number of Conservative friends (and Liberal enemies), not least from his position as Clerk to the Tendring Hundred Railway. Moreover, as the *eminence grise* behind the Gas Consumers Company in 1866, he might claim a special interest. Lastly, there was Henry Jones.[20]

There were few more remarkable figures in Victorian Colchester than Henry Jones, the son of Jesse Jones, a hero of the Napoleonic Wars who, shot clean through at the Battle of Waterloo, lived to tell the tale – many times – and exhibit the offending bullet to the citizens of Colchester where he settled. Here Jesse Jones raised three sons who grew up widely exercising those high spirits that had made their father a hero. A string of petty court appearances involving poaching, illegal fishing, the sale of nobbled horses, punch-ups, inebriation and 'furious driving' marked their progress from adolescence to manhood. Henry Jones however added to a pugnacious temperament a sharp mind and an ability to talk himself out of almost any situation. Articled to the law, he soon developed a flourishing private practice and became renowned throughout the Eastern Counties for his aggressive court room style. He also developed a taste for business. His most productive side-line was a large brickworks to the north of Colchester from which he built many houses in the area and played a significant part in the development of the 'New Town' district. His legal skills and business acumen he now concentrated in a furious attack upon the Gas Company's Bill.[21]

It should be noted that this formidable quartet of citizens fully carried both the town and the Borough Council by the force if not the facts of their argument. The Gas Company, they protested, were taking advantage of a temporary phenomenon – high coal prices – to secure a 25% increase in their maximum price for gas, an enormous rise, considering that the whole matter had been argued out in the town so recently as 1866. No railway company would be permitted to do this by Parliament. The real problem was that the Company was grossly overcapitalised, putting a nominal value of £37,000 on its elderly plant, when a new gasworks could be built from scratch for £20,000. Colchester was thus being asked to pay for the mistakes of the Company in days gone by in order to provide dividends for its present shareholders.

These claims were not so far off the mark, as Harvey freely confessed when writing some years later. What probably hardened opinion in the Council, if not the town at large, was the refusal of the Gas Company to consider a compromise figure which, under the threat of a rival company and a contested Bill, they had so readily conceded nine years before. Great play was also made of their refusal to allow public access to their accounts. Such a move would of course be unthinkable by normal 19th century business practice, but it did tactically emphasise that the public good was not the sole object of a limited liability company, that the Gas Company might well have something to hide.[22]

Indeed they did. Anxious to ascertain the strength of their case in going thus to Parliament, the Board had turned for assistance to Jabez Church, himself once the lessee of the Gasworks, whose proposal 30 years before that they should seek incorporation was now fully vindicated. Church's review of the Company's books revealed serious discrepancies in the coal account that could not all be blamed on the recent dismissal of their Manager. This disturbing information, however, was no longer secret.

For what neither Henry Jones nor John Bawtree Harvey mentioned publicly was that the Gas Company's Parliamentary Bill was discussed, devised and drawn up, clause by clause, by their solicitors, Turner and Deane, the senior partner of whom was Sayers Turner, Town Clerk of Colchester. The borough's decision to oppose the Bill rendered this impartial public servant the legal advisor to both sides. Privy to all the Gas Company's plans, Messrs. Turner and Deane withdrew their services to become chief advisors to the opposition. Thus when the Bill's opponents demanded so stridently to see the Company's books and the Gas Company refused, both sides actually knew the current situation. And lest there should be any doubt, the Gas Company's late Manager, dismissed only some 18 months previously, returned to Colchester, freely advising the town on the weakness of the Gas Company's case.[23]

It is surely significant that Harvey and his Directors now chose to place their affairs in the hands of Henry Goody, the senior active Liberal solicitor of the town. Goody also happened to be the Clerk and legal adviser to the Commissioners and Harvey's close nonconformist colleague and relative by marriage. Thus, resting in part as they did on old political antagonisms, both sides were well entrenched when the Bill came before a Committee of the House of Commons.

First came the Gas Company's evidence, a case largely prepared by Harvey himself. Colchester Corporation, however, refused to reply because, as they later claimed, the Parliamentary Committee contained members known to be biased in favour of gas companies. Their case untested, the borough nonetheless went on to the greater expense of a contest in the House of Lords, urged on by the confident Henry Jones. Such resolve created sufficient alarm for a petition to be presented, signed by 163 ratepayers, several of them influential figures in the town, protesting at the great expense that this involved. Their alarm was justified. In the event practically the entire Gas Bill was carried in the Lords, at costs to the Gas Company of £2,167 and to the ratepayers of just under £1,200.[24]

That the whole proceedings were a triumph for Bawtree Harvey, if not for the book-keeping of the Gas Company, is underlined by a little ceremony conducted shortly afterwards, when the grateful shareholders presented him with a cash donation of 100 guineas, the same sum as he had earlier been presented by the entire town for half a lifetime of public service. That the tension of these events also left deep scars is illustrated by a remarkable outburst Harvey committed to a private journal. Entitled "The Opponents of the Colchester Gas Amendment Act, 1875", its tone is decidedly biblical, reading like some Old Testament triumph of the Children of Israel over the Philistines, a literature with which Harvey, as a leading nonconformist, was most familiar. It also implies that rather more was at stake in 1875 than the public record suggests.

This "insignificant faction", writes Harvey, meaning, presumably, Henry Jones, Sayers Turner, Charlie Hawkins and all, "whose reverses made them pitiable", were openly set on bringing the Gas Company to "confusion and ruin".

> "They inaugurated a special mission to destroy. But the Company with a marvellous tenacity of life has survived the attacks of their enemies . . . They trusted to their skill to knock the Company on the head, but only succeeded in inflicting some tremendous wounds on the pocket of the public".[25]

This was an extraordinary outpouring for a man whose sagacity and genial humour made him the object of great respect within the town. Fortunately, he also left a more typical footnote that any knowing reader might enjoy. During his retirement Harvey compiled scrapbooks of press cuttings chronicling the public events with which he had been involved. In one corner he pasted a law report from 40 years before. It records in telling detail how a young law clerk, much the worse for drink, had punched the policeman who arrested him, argued all the way to the cell, fighting three policemen as he went; and even argued the next morning with the Bench, until threatened with being put in the stocks. It was none other than the youthful Henry Jones.[26]

There were however public reasons, other than ancient antagonisms, for attacking the 1875 Gas Bill. One was the possibility of municipal ownership, a practice increasingly being adopted in larger towns. The point was put quite bluntly by James Paxman, one of the most outspoken opponents of the Bill, in this his first major essay into the public affairs of the town. Addressing the earlier Public Meeting and anticipating (incorrectly) the Public Health Act due to be passed later that year, he said

> "Probably before long the Council would have to take over the gas and water supply, and if the Company obtained power to increase their price for gas, it would enable them to put a larger value upon the property, and the town would then have to pay £10,000 or £15,000 more . . ."

This was precisely the dilemma of municipal ownership. For as the Gas Company's new solicitor, Henry Goody, quickly pointed out, it was no good Henry Jones talking about new gasworks being built for £20,000. Parliament would require the borough to purchase the present works at a fair valuation. This was currently put at £37,000.

Were they prepared to pay that?[27]

No one answered Henry Goody. The question was in any case rhetorical. For most of the citizens present, including perhaps Henry Goody, probably agreed with Henry Jones on the real value of the Gasworks.

Thus were the arguments rehearsed in 1875 for an undertaking soon to convulse the town. The only difference was this: it was not the Gasworks that were to be at stake.

E for ELECTORS, so easily led,
   Who, it's hoped, will believe everything
     that is said
There may be, of course, disappointment in
     store,
But *that* won't be new, for they've felt it
     before.

6

1870-1878: Graveyards and Fires

Even while the contest over the 1875 Gas Bill was taking place, there was a growing opinion among members of the Borough Council that the Waterworks should come under municipal control. Two factors, each in its own way a matter of life and death, made water a more serious issue than gas. One was Public Health. The other was the risk of fire.

Probably more by good fortune than any change of policy, the town had for nearly 20 years been spared a major conflagration such as had raged near the top of Head Street for three days over Christmas 1834, and at the top of High Street in 1842, destroying the line of properties beyond the Fire Office. By 1873 the central urban area was much more densely built on and commercial properties were of greater extent and value. In December of that year the inevitable occurred. A major fire destroyed three leading business premises including the printers Benham and Harrisons, the virtual owners of the *Essex Standard* since Taylor had left the town.[1]

In the inquest that followed, much criticism was directed at the existing fire plugs and their clumsy handling by the volunteer fire brigade, a body of worthies recently established by the Essex and Suffolk Fire Office. This distinguished and successful organisation, operating from its colonnaded headquarters at the top of the High Street, had for 70 years provided a unique service to the town in case of fire. Not only did they for many years possess the only effective fire fighting equipment, but they undertook to bring it into action regardless of whether properties insured by them were involved. More recently they had added to their hand-pumped 'engines' the sophistication of a fire escape which, leaning against the wall of old St Runwald's church, was regularly manhandled by the volunteers.[2]

However neither additional training for the fire brigade nor the replacement of fire plugs that were primarily designed for watering the roads was of any value without a steady supply of water. This was the problem that dominated discussion. For although the Waterworks maintained an open reservoir on the old site inside the Balkerne Gate, at the same elevation as the High Street, pressure was required to move the water on. In the middle of the night that pressure could only be provided by starting up the company's steam engine at the bottom of Balkerne Hill. This in turn put the Waterworks to the considerable expense of keeping their engine fired-up at night in case it should be needed. For 30 years the Essex and Suffolk, although strictly a private, not a public, body had paid the Waterworks an annual retainer of £20 for this service and for the water used in any fire. Was £20 enough? Peter Bruff thought not, considering the extension of the water mains in the past 30 years. Was £20 worth paying? The Fire Office was not sure; particularly now that the 1872 Public Health Act laid upon the Borough Council the obligation of providing water in case of fire, an obligation which, interestingly enough, was also written, in identical wording, into the Commissioners' 1847 Act. The Fire Office therefore withheld their £20. The Waterworks now calculated that water pumped at night would cost them £150 a year. Impasse. Meanwhile a large consignment of new fire hydrants sat useless in a shed, pending an agreement.

All this was bad news for the harrassed Chairman of the Essex and Suffolk Fire Office – Charles Henry Hawkins. He now faced a conflict of interests indeed. As Chairman of the Fire Office, he was distinctly against fires; as leader of the Conservative majority on the Town Council and "permanent" Chairman of the Sanitary Committee, he could not let matters fester unresolved; as advisor to his late brother's widow, who owned half the Waterworks, he did not wish to see that company discredited. With considerable energy and (of course) obvious concern for the public good, he set out to square the triangle.

His first attempt in 1874 foundered on the inability of the three sides to agree on methods and charges. Nor were they helped by ambiguities in the 1872 Act that left it unclear how far the Commissioners still held their old responsibilities. In 1877 (and two fires later) Hawkins made another determined effort. A committee of the district's leading citizens was formed, and an agreement – of sorts – was reached: £40 a year to the Waterworks plus five shillings for each of the new hydrants. These were soon to be tested. In November a fire at the back of the Cups Hotel spread to the foundry next door, largely because of the difficulty of getting water. In the following January the new Castle Brewery was engulfed, but the horrible climax came on the night of February 15th.[3]

About eight o'clock that evening smoke was seen curling above the door of 36, High Street, the millinery shop of Mr Curdling, who had left for his home in Maldon Road half an hour before. With commendable speed the police from the Town Hall opposite brought out their reel hose, while Mr Curdling was sent for. By good fortune there was a hydrant in the road opposite his shop and in front of St

CHARLES HENRY HAWKINS, four times mayor of Colchester, ponders his master plan for eliminating the fire hazards of Colchester without eliminating his sister-in-law, his business partner and the Conservative majority on the Council.

Runwald's church. The hose was fixed. No water came. Another hydrant in East Stockwell Street was tried. No water. Mr Curdling arrived. A runner was sent to the Waterworks at the bottom of Balkerne Hill. By one of those cruel twists of fate a telegraphic wire between the Police Station and the Waterworks was due to be fixed that week. Crowds gathered, watching in helpless fascination as the flames leapt up, spreading to the fancy toy store at No. 35 and Pocock's boot and shoe shop at No. 37. The Fire Brigade had now assembled. Still no water. Very rude comments were passed about the Waterworks. Mr Staines at No. 38 owned a large draper's store. Most of his assistants were now at hand, organising a chain of buckets from a nearby well. At last water was secured from a hydrant in Culver Street and directed with great effect by Mr Quilter using the police hose from the top of his house at No. 39. Meanwhile the fire had reached The Colchester Bazaar at No. 34.

It needs some imagination to recreate the public impact and the visual effect of such a fire in a pre-electric, pre-cinema society. The blaze would be visible from every corner of the town and far into the country, illuminating with unnatural brightness the animated scene below: the growing crowds of bystanders, the shouted instructions from the several interested parties, the arrival of soldiers from the barracks to render manly aid, the despairing shopkeeper seeing his whole stock and livelihood consumed by fire or saturated with water. For water was at last obtained from the hydrant opposite the blaze, 35 minutes after the alarm had been raised. Long into the night they continued to fight the fire.

The recriminations that followed with the dawn can easily be imagined. It took more than a letter to the press to restore Bruff's credibility. Water *was* different from gas. Nor were matters improved by the revelation that the 35 minute delay in raising water was caused by the service pipe to the St Runwald's hydrant being "unaccountably turned off".[4] This only emphasised the chief shortcoming of the current system: it had no current. For although Bruff had worked energetically in the last few years to increase the number of water sources, to extend the mains and to install new engines and pumps, water was still only supplied for a certain number of hours a day. Great arguments existed over how many hours. In fact it depended where you lived. For the streets of Colchester were divided up into zones, and by a series of turncocks, operated manually by Waterworks' employees, a whole zone would be cut off so that another could be supplied. And this was only during the daytime. No running water was supplied in the evening or at night, the very occasion when virtually all fires occurred.

Naked flames were universal in Victorian times and wood was a major building material. Gas lamps, oil lamps, candle ends, workmen's braziers and dying embers, falling over, caught by the wind or left forgotten had all played their part in a string of expensive bonfires that one estimate costed at £25,000. You could get a new gasworks for that. Maybe you could get a new waterworks too. Or maybe you could so improve the present one that it would provide a constant supply: water under pressure out of a tap or out of a hydrant for 24 hours a day –

An eye-witness painting of the High Street fire of 1842. Water pumped by the Essex & Suffolk fire engine plays on the building opposite. The colonnaded Fire Office at the top of High Street survives unscathed, its entire walls, then and now, being coated with plates of cast iron.

and night. This was the ideal that had been talked about since 1847 and the means to obtain it had been talked about for almost as long. The Borough Surveyor, Joseph Hope, had suggested it when he first came to the town 25 years before; Harvey had outlined it in 1858; the Commissioners had made scale drawings. It was a 60-foot water-tower on Balkerne Hill. It would cost £3,000. Once more the idea was urged and the suggestion made that the borough, the Fire Office and the Waterworks Company might contribute £1,000 each. But that was before the fire at Mr Curdling's. That changed the mood. Bawtree Harvey might lament Bruff's failure to provide fresh water to the Hythe, but the health of the poor did not directly concern the merchant community unless there was an epidemic or, worse still, a rise in the rates. But Bruff's failure to provide against a High Street fire, in which innocent retailers suffered alike with the guilty, was quite another matter. Within a week the Town Clerk wrote a fateful letter. However, before we learn its contents, we must reconsider that rather more despised aspect of the water problem, environmental health.[5]

In most respects the situation in Colchester had not changed since the Commissioners had completed their main drainage system in 1854, an assertion borne out by a stationary death rate in the decades that followed. The appropriately named Inspector of Nuisances continued to nose out the worst abuses at the rate of nearly 200 cases a year. Since this was a statistic used to justify his existence, it is difficult to be sure how far it reflects the zeal of the Inspector, how far the continued dirtiness of Colchester, but there are good reasons for believing the latter.

For example, in 1865 the doctors of the town, disturbed by the spread of the latest cholera epidemic and its possible arrival in Colchester, had undertaken a survey of the environmental state of the borough without, somewhat to Harvey's pique, involving the Commissioners in their fieldwork. Their lengthy final report, transcribed verbatim in the local press, carries this revealing introduction:

"The visits we paid were welcomed by the inhabitants who, living among scenes of filth and nuisance almost untold and intolerable, seemed to hope that at last some prospect was open to them of getting the sanitary state of their premises and neighbourhoods corrected, and that at last, though late, their landlord would be compelled, by some new effort on the part of those in power, to do their duty to the tenants. In many cases they said that the "Commissioners man" had been there some years or months ago, and had seen the places and perhaps verbally condemned them, said they should be remedied, and that was the last they had heard of the matter till the present state of filth had grown up."

The detailed review that follows, couched in that lurid language which, probably with justice, 19th-century sanitary reports invariably used, leaves little doubt that the worst abuses of the 1840s were still widespread. A few quotations will suffice:

The Streets
"in no other town in England, we believe, of corresponding size is so much manure, straw and filth lying about".

Water Supply
"the urgency for an extension of wholesome water is now as great as it was when the Water Company first was started at a time when Colchester was a far smaller town . . ."
". . . as medical men we have at times heard the appeal of a sick and fevered child to its mother for drink postponed until the water cart should arrive".

Cess Pits
". . . plots of land, honeycombed with cesspits to an extent utterly incredible . . .";
". . . there are everywhere large accumulations of privy soil, and from the multiplication of privies a state of things has come about too horrible to be talked about".

Courtyards
". . . pig styes containing 20 pigs fed on butchers'
offal . . ."
"a brick pit containing privy accumulation sufficient to
drown a man in at the back of the house, stinking and
polluting the air of the neighbourhood";
"*Bakers Row, Magdalen Street:* One open privy close to a
building, another draining into a neighbouring garden,
very offensive, without cover. Pigs kept, 10. Inhabitants,
63. Three privies only; no water supply".[6]

This catalogue of sanitary horror might make disturbing reading
now, but it could have been written any time between 1840 and 1880.
It is, moreover, difficult to discover one tangible improvement that
ensued as a result of the Doctors' Report, even though they were at
times sharply critical of the Commissioners. Peter Bruff was at his
most elusive at this date, cholera did not extend its hand into the
borough, and the doctors soon returned to their practices. Indeed,
given that they had their own professional association in the town, the
doctors of Colchester exhibited remarkably little collective zeal in the
sanitary cause. With the honourable exception of Dr Williams, there
were few individual initiatives either. Why was this?

Partly it was because doctors were not yet regarded as public
servants in the modern sense. Environmental health they considered
the province of the Commissioners. Moreover aside from the
unlucrative and part-time posts of medical advisers to the hospital or
to the workhouse, local doctors depended for their livelihood on fee-
paying customers. While making allowances for sick clubs and the
desperation of serious illness, this still meant that their services were
largely confined to the more affluent classes. Not least among the skills
required for this was a bedside manner, as respect for the profession
grew, and as doctors came to share with the clergy the task of offering
comfort, amelioration and explanation to the sick and dying. Cures
were harder to come by. The key to this bedside manner was
confidentiality. Doctors were frequently sworn to secrecy by their
middle class customers. Tradesmen in particular were anxious to keep
from general knowledge any kind of contagious illness, for fear of the
disastrous consequences this might have upon their trade.[7] Middle
class opinion was now very sensitive to the dangerous potential of
infectious disease, not least because of a continued uncertainty about
its precise causation and the specific means of its transmission. This
in turn points to another reason for public caution among the medical
profession. Amid petty jealousies and keen competition for the
restricted fee-paying market, many doctors were unwilling either to
agree or to disagree in public, or to be dogmatic outside their surgery,
preferring the omniscience they enjoyed among their own patients.

No such reservations however troubled Dr Bree, particularly over the Balkerne "Pesthouse".

Edinburgh-trained, Bree eloped with and married the daughter of a baronet, settling in Colchester in 1859 as Physician to the Essex and Colchester Hospital. His social standing and natural inclinations drew him into public life, where he became both a county magistrate and a member of the Commissioners. Like several Colchester doctors he had a passion for natural history and gained a minor national reputation in the subject. He was, for a while, an editor of *The Naturalist.* A resolute churchman, he published a best-seller refuting Darwinism and was at all times a man of trenchant opinion. He also clung with much tenacity to the view that disease could be carried airborne over quite prodigious distances. He was therefore quick to protest when the Board of Guardians, responsible for the running of the Workhouse, built their isolation wards adjacent to the main premises and close to a row of 18 cottages on Balkerne Hill. Nor was Bree moved by the information that several other towns had similar arrangements, or that the site had been approved by the Chief Medical Officer of the Local Government Board. No one had consulted Dr Bree or Dr Laver, the local Poor Law Medical Officer. Protest turned to righteous indignation when the smallpox epidemic of 1871-72 reached Colchester. No sooner were cases confined to the isolation wards than the disease appeared in the 18 cottages nearby. In all, ten cases were recorded there. This confidential information Bree only secured by writing personally to every doctor in the town for details of the smallpox cases they had treated. Even so, at least one doctor was not prepared to give the details of his patients. Bree was able to plot 87 out of over 100 cases recorded in Colchester and 13 subsequent deaths, four in the Workhouse itself. By counting all the cases in St Peter's and St Martin's parishes, he was ready to attribute 45 of the

DR. CHARLES ROBERT BREE (1811-1886), author of 'Fallacies of Darwinism' and for 22 years Physician to the Essex and Colchester Hospital, fulminating against the Balkerne Hill Pesthouse. An enthusiastic bird watcher, his remarkable sightings of North American species in the Colchester area are no longer recognised by ornithology.

total to the "Pesthouse" source. While we might have difficulty today in sharing the doctor's confidence, we might also hold a different view of the running of an isolation hospital. Bree's enquiries revealed that the infected patients were regularly visited by ordinary Workhouse inmates, an obvious explanation for the spread of the infection there.[8]

The 1872 smallpox outbreak in Colchester also sheds interesting light on that unique example of 19th-century medical compulsion, the requirement, credited with greatly curtailing the disease, that all babies should be vaccinated against smallpox within three months of birth. As a result of the 1871-72 outbreak, fines for evading this measure were increased and every Board of Guardians was compelled to appoint a Vaccination Officer. In 1872, in the same week as he was expounding his smallpox findings to the Colchester Board of Guardians, Dr Bree found himself as a member of the County Bench hearing a case brought against two citizens of Brightlingsea by the local Vaccination Officer. In his prosecution the officer explained that Brightlingsea people were strongly opposed to compulsory vaccination, and since this was only performed one day in every three months, they usually contrived to have whooping cough, measles or some other ailment on the day concerned. Hence this resort to the law. The first defendant, a shoemaker, protested that having taken his child on the day prescribed, the local doctor had told him to wait until "another time" as he "hadn't any stuff". Others in court confirmed this explanation. Dr Bree, clearly astounded at such ramshackle arrangements, dismissed the case, pointing out that there was little purpose in such prosecutions being brought. The Vaccination Officer, who took this personally, retorted that the arrangements were not laid down by him, but by the Board of Guardians. Moreover, he observed laconically, Brightlingsea people were very fortunate; elsewhere in the Lexden and Winstree district vaccinations were only performed one day in every six months.

Although subsequently hotly disputed, such insights into the working of 19th-century bureaucracy in a rural area should temper any extreme claims made for the efficacy of compulsory vaccination. They certainly provide explanation for the regular but muted reappearance of the disease into the 20th century. Moreover, as Dr Bree also pointed out, vaccination was only really reliable if a regular programme of periodic revaccination was conducted, and this, outside the armed forces, was nowhere consistently followed.[9]

The dismissal of the Brightlingsea case also illustrates the relative vindictiveness of the Coggeshall magistrates towards the radical working class leader, John Castle, Secretary of the Coggeshall Cooperative Society and (far worse in the eyes of the magistrates) the local sponsor of Joseph Arch, the agricultural trade union leader. On grounds of conscience and because a relation's child had died as a consequence, Castle refused to have his own children vaccinated.

Eighteen times he was dragged into court and fined a total of more than £20. Even though some of his fines were met by the Anti-Vaccination League this sum probably represented four months' wages to John Castle.[10]

As for the people of Brightlingsea who had opposed vaccination, it is unlikely that they were so high-minded or so persecuted. Suspicion of authority and a respect for old superstitions were more likely explanations for their attitude. Had Dr Bree been a member of the Colchester Bench he would that same week have heard the case of Mrs Cocker. She wanted to bring her neighbours to court for assault, but was too poor to risk preferring charges. Mrs Cocker had contracted smallpox and, as was apparently standard practice, another woman had brought her baby to catch the smallpox from Mrs Cocker. The baby had died and Mrs Cocker had got the blame. It seems probable that such crude and backstreet remedies continued to operate for many years among the poor, far from the attention of Dr Bree, let alone the Balkerne Pesthouse.[11]

The question of the isolation hospital was in any case to prove not simply a matter of medical opinion. It soon became a text-book case of narrow legalisms between established authorities. True, somewhat late in the day, a makeshift metal shed was installed at the far side of the Workhouse gardens as an alternative to the Pesthouse. But, as it now abutted a public footpath, Bree considered the site no better. Gaunt and impracticable, the building was in practice little used in the following decade.

Bree's own proposal was more reasonable and far-sighted. He recommended joint action by the Board of Guardians, the Commissioners and the Borough Council, assisted if necessary by the Essex and Colchester Hospital, to build a true isolation hospital on a site sufficiently far from other habitation. Such a proposal however fell foul of the difficulty Victorians faced in housing paupers and ordinary citizens on the same premises, particularly when they all had fever. The question dragged on long after Dr Bree had retired and left the town, sinking to the lowest level of parish pump politics. The Board of Guardians, adhering strictly to the ruling of the Local Government Board, their masters, refused to make provision for any but contagious paupers and the Borough Council, seeking to cater for the rest of the population, cast around for a suitable site for an isolation hospital of their own which would not have disastrous consequences for adjacent land and property values. Several sites were considered, most of them rejected by the outcry from their potential neighbours. Finally a detached farmhouse at Myland was chosen on the borough-owned Severalls estate. But still one obstacle remained. The town's Medical Officer of Health, Dr Finch, convinced that a permanent hospital was an unnecessary extravagance, recommended instead the purchase of a few tents to be kept as occasional accommodation for the suitably infected. Only in 1884 was the Myland farmhouse finally opened, a site which the hospital still occupies today.[12]

There were of course other theories apart from Dr Bree's about the contagious potential of Balkerne Hill. Standing a short distance from the Pesthouse and the large Waterworks reservoir inside the Balkerne Gate was the churchyard of St Mary-at-the-Walls. Shortly before the arrival of the smallpox outbreak this received the suspicious attention of our aged legal friend, Fred Philbrick.[13] The church, where Philip Morant had once ministered, had just acquired a new incumbent, the Rev. Canon Irvine, an outspoken and energetic man. He early appreciated that this most fashionable parish required better facilities for worship than the plain brick structure that had been put up 160 years before, following the church's destruction in the Siege of Colchester. Irvine decided on a new and larger building, the footings for which extended into the ancient graveyard. Naturally the bishop's permission was secured and every care was taken to provide a seemly reburial for those ancient bones and modern coffins that were uncovered lying in a family vault. The workmen concerned even used disinfectant. But it was August and hot and, as the old earth was dug over, a musty smell arose. At this point it reached the sensitive nose of Dr Finch, at that date one of the town's general practitioners. Finch was then tending several cases of dysentery in cottages on Balkerne Hill, so soon to be threatened by Pesthouse small-pox. One dysentery patient died. Then Finch himself felt ill. Immediately he realised that the source of fever was the contaminated graveyard soil. As if a medieval plague had descended, he advised a number of his patients nearby to flee their houses. He also warned Fred Philbrick whose son, Horace, the erstwise solicitor to the Gas Consumers Company, lived in St Mary's Cottage on the far side of the graveyard. Even though Horace Philbrick had left for a

FREDERICK BLOMFIELD PHIL-BRICK distinctly bemused by the behaviour of the Gas Company, the Home Office Medical Department and the owners of the Waterworks.

seaside holiday, his father, never one to understate his case, wrote to Gladstone's Home Secretary, H.A. Bruce to warn him of these awful happenings. The following morning a second death occurred on Balkerne Hill and Philbrick, as he later put it, "not having heard from the Secretary of State", telegraphed this vital information to Downing Street. Nineteenth-century statesmen were tolerably used to eccentric correspondents, but one wonders what Bruce made of Philbrick's telegraph. Possibly the lurid references in his letter to "exhuming bodies" prompted Bruce to send a Home Office Medical Inspector to ascertain what sort of an emergency the nation faced. One also wonders what the Inspector, Mr Holland, made of Colchester. A swift visit to the graveyard reassured him. The site was covered and, but for a large mound of excavated soil, quite unremarkable. No corpses, no stench. With characteristic tact he opened his official enquiry by suggesting that the extreme heat of August had perhaps enlivened the earthy smell, but he doubted whether any illness had resulted. In fact his visit was now monumentally unnecessary, but the insight his Enquiry gives into public attitudes in Colchester leaves us all indebted to Frederick Philbrick.

Viewed in one light the proceedings approached high comedy. Philbrick and Dr Finch cut a sorry sight when it was shown that the houses afflicted with diarrhoea ("cholernic dysentery", said Philbrick) were sixty yards from the churchyard where twelve able-bodied labourers under the Clerk of Works had toiled in the heat of the sun "exhuming bodies" without any ill effect. On the other hand, the infected cottages all had backyard privies up against the Roman wall which stank to heaven and, on the evidence of the Sanitary Inspector, were only emptied twice a year, in spring and autumn. Their drains were not much better either. Moreover it was soon shown that similar cases of diarrhoea and dysentery occurred throughout the town, particularly in the summer months, far from St Mary's graveyard.

But if Dr Finch's suspicions of the churchyard soil were (so to speak) quite groundless, it is also clear that the majority of those worthies present at the Enquiry, key figures in the public health of Colchester, still shared the 'miasmatic' view that smell was the primary agent of disease, even though evidence supporting the alternative 'germ' theory of disease, and pointing to the probability of specific causal organisms active in contaminated water, had now been demonstrated in a number of national investigations. Only the government inspector came close to suggesting that all the dysentery and summer diarrhoea of Colchester might come from food or water contaminated by sewage. Yet even he was miasmist enough to write in his subsequent report:

"Many of the poor . . . keep their water in pails or cans, when if imperfectly covered . . . the water may absorb any foulness in the air, and it is well known that many cases of intestinal disorder in various forms have been excited by water originally pure becoming so contaminated".

Much attention was therefore focused at the Enquiry on the smell from drains and sewers in the town and the need for these to have ventilation to dispel the fumes. One discomfort consequent upon installing water closets, 500 of which, it was claimed, had in the last few years replaced outhouse privies, was a tendency for sewer gas to issue from them and pervade the house. The Town Surveyor, Joseph Hope, considered that they actually led to an increase in the death rate compared to privies, the smell from which could be subdued by throwing weeds and pea shells on top. Although sharply contradicted by Mr Holland, such a view expressed by an official so closely involved with the borough's health was hardly reassuring.

There was of course a further attraction to an outhouse privy which Bawtree Harvey once more underlined. Large numbers of citizens still regarded their contents as a source of profit to be sold to local farmers' men – though not in August when the harvest found them otherwise employed. Since the contents of cesspits and privies were (quite literally) the owner's property, the Commissioners could only intervene when a public nuisance was proved. Harvey illustrated the difficulties this presented by an anecdote. On one occasion

> "The Inspector of Nuisances reported a nuisance . . . in a court in Magdalen Street, and on going to the spot the next day found it had been removed. He went to the house intending to praise the people for their prompt compliance . . ., and, on the door being opened, found that it had been moved into the house where the family were living".

Harvey also made sure that the limitations of Colchester's water supply were recorded, and gave the Inspector details of those areas unsupplied by the Waterworks. Though he was careful to avoid criticisms of the Waterworks Company, it may well have been Harvey's influence which led the Inspector to stress in his written report the unsatisfactory nature of the present intermittent supply and the need for water to be constantly available from the tap.

In fact the state of affairs on Balkerne Lane sufficiently concerned the Inspector that he extended his Enquiry to a second visit. This enabled him to meet Dr Bree. Bree expounded upon a number of points, expressing the opinion that smallpox infection could travel unaided through the air over a mile and a half. In fairness to the doctor this claim was based on a pamphlet by William Budd, one of the pioneers of germ theory, whose investigations are today invariably upheld as models of their kind. Bree had of course raised the question of the Pesthouse and a conversation of music hall confusion followed when Mr Holland thought that Dr Bree from his colourful language was talking about some adjacent pig styes. These often abutted 19th-century workhouses, where the pigs invariably grew very sleek from a steady diet of inedible slops rejected by the workhouse paupers.

Fred Philbrick did not attend Mr Holland's second Enquiry. He wrote instead:

> "Sir,
>   As you treated me on the former occasion with marked contempt, and as you refused my application for an adjournment (he had asked for this in order to bring his son back from the seaside to give evidence), I decline to take part in any further proceedings in which you may be called to preside".

Thus put in his place the government inspector returned to London. Only one other aspect of his visit needs to be discussed – perhaps the most significant. Those 500 additional water closets which the surveyor regarded with such suspicion represented a sanitary revolution that would increasingly transfer attention (as well as sewage) from the privies to the river.

In 1871 Colchester possessed some 5,000 houses. According to Holland's written report only one tenth of them boasted a water closet and many of these fed not into the sewers but into cess pits. Thus if the figure of 500 is reliable, even after making allowance for multiple residences (the Census of 1871 recorded 5,387 'families'), the water closet must have been very scarce in Colchester before 1870. Moreover the tone of Holland's report and such statistics as are available for large cities imply that one water closet to nine privies was a poor ratio for that date.[14] The evidence therefore suggests a recent and rapid increase in the number of W.C.s, an increase that would accelerate as the 1870s progressed and Colchester caught up with much of urban Britain.

Such rapid sanitary progress would of course place great responsibility upon the comprehensive system of main sewers which, constructed so carefully between 1847 and 1854 from the Commissioners' meagre resources, now discharged in ever growing volume into the river at four places between North Bridge and the Hythe. Given that the Colne was dammed at two points by watermills and was tidal from there onwards, the consequences were obvious. No elver had more difficult a journey than did the sewage of Colchester to reach the sea. In hot weather when the water was low, it accumulated in alarming proportions along that pretty riverside walk between North Bridge and Middle Mill. It almost discouraged naked youths from sporting in

Chopping's millpond and offering predictable suggestions to the girls at the silk factory. If it did not clog in the weir, it continued in slow progress to the tidal basin at East Mills. Here it made little advance before the next incoming tide swept it back and deposited it on the mud at high water mark. The miller Edward Marriage protested that he had been forced to evacuate his house in the mill and to remove some 500 tons of sewage from the basin. Even if his new house was somewhat grander, and a good deal of the 500 tons was river mud, removed to facilitate the arrival of barges at the mill, this was still a telling criticism. From the mid-1860s, in fact, complaints about the river had been growing, corroborated by the Registrar General's report of 1866 that fever invariably was found in houses unfortunate enough to be beside it.[15]

Why had the Commissioners not acted? It is interesting to note Bawtree Harvey's comments, expressed both at meetings of that body and at the St Mary's graveyard Enquiry. Firstly, the Commissioners had no money to install new sewers, having already gone to the limit of their borrowing power to improve the navigation. Secondly, they had for many years been expecting government legislation that would compel local authorities to meet certain drainage standards. If they acted prematurely, all their works might be invalidated by these regulations.

Setting aside the obvious pretext this provided for inaction, there were good reasons for this claim. Harvey prided himself on his detailed knowledge of national legislation and administrative trends, based partly on a close reading of the national press and partly on information received from his eldest son who was successively a junior official at the Treasury and a leading London banker. In particular Harvey would be well aware of the controversy that had followed Edwin Chadwick's obsession in the 1840s with the universal desirability of glazed egg-shaped sewage pipes. If Colchester again installed brick-built barrel drains, national legislation might require their subsequent removal. Indeed it is a paradox of the Public Health Movement that while central initiative and compulsory legislation were constantly resisted in the name of local autonomy, local authorities constantly waited on central initiative. At least this is true of Colchester. The alternative of a private Act of Parliament had, as we have seen, an unhappy and expensive history in the borough. Many times during these decades Commissioners and Councillors either postponed action because some 'general measure' was shortly expected from Parliament or urged action on some permissive clause in the belief that it was soon to become obligatory.[16]

This is exemplified in the question of the river, where national legislation did indeed prove to be the catalyst of change. The Pollution of Rivers Act of 1876 could, as its name implied, provide

legal redress for citizens who
sought to dissuade a local
authority or industrial concern
from pouring effluent into a
river. Even before it was opera-
tional, this fact was pointed out
in no uncertain terms in a
trenchant letter to the Colchester press that marked the
entry into public life of Wilson
Marriage, son of Edward, one of
the ablest of a new generation of
Colchester's industrialists.[17]

This combination of public
protest and legal liability now
drove the Borough Council into
action. Having so recently entered into their new obligations
under the Public Health Act,
their response was rather hesi-
tant. Initially they commissioned a report from a London
engineer, Mr Bailey Denton. He
recommended an outlay of
£25,000 on new sewers and the
purchase of 50 acres for a

*WILSON MARRIAGE averts his gaze
from the 500 tons of sewage allegedly
accumulated at East Mills.*

sewage farm. Partly intimidated by the cost, partly aware that several
ambitious sewage schemes elsewhere in Britain had proved expensive
failures, the Town Council put the matter before a public meeting of
the town, a method of direct democracy still practised in these years,
though not always with felicitous results. Predictably there were
grumblings about the cost and misgivings about the outcome. With
some relief Denton's report was shelved and the subject for a while
abandoned. One cannot help feeling that both the town and the
Council were still reeling over their defeat in the Gas Amendment Bill
three months before. Thus a further year passed.[18]

The Pollution of Rivers Act now became law and the Local
Government Board itself continually drew the borough's attention to
the problem. The Council therefore set up a sub-committee of three
to investigate the sewage question. It was chaired by the mayor for that
year, Philip Oxenden Papillon, Lord of the Manor of Lexden. Entering
his inheritance in 1858, Papillon had for a time served as an M.P. for
Colchester, succeeding the ailing William Hawkins. However his
unpopular High Church stance and his family's limited financial
resources soon led him to lower his sights and turn to municipal office
instead. Spared the indignity of an elected post, he was given an

aldermanic chair, becoming one of that inner Tory group who effectively controlled the Corporation. Though still a relatively young man he was accelerated to the chair of Lexden and Winstree Bench over the head of the long-serving Charles Henry Hawkins, a snub which this experienced politician accepted as part of the social order, though clearly it rankled at the time. Meanwhile Papillon's financial well-being was much improved by the conversion into a housing complex of the Lord's Land Estate over whose fields the water pipes had run from the Town Water House 250 years before. By a fine historic irony the new roads of artisan dwellings, built in a grid around Papillon Road, became once more the subject of dispute, remaining for years without proper lighting or paving while the ground landlord, Alderman Papillon, remained in conflict with the Urban Sanitary Authority (i.e. the Borough Council) over their requirement that the roads should be put into a fit state of repair before they were adopted.[19]

Papillon's report on the sewerage problem, delivered in January 1877, was at first sight an impressive document. Accompanied by the Borough Surveyor, the sub-committee had visited in succession the sewerage schemes at Edmonton, Coventry, Rugby, Wimbledon, Croydon and Tottenham. They had attended a conference in London, organised by the Society of Arts on "Health and Sewerage in Towns", and held a long interview with the consulting engineer of the Local Government Board on current plans for Maidstone, a town whose size and circumstance closely resembled Colchester. All this suggests thoroughness. However it also emerged from Alderman Papillon's six-point recommendations that five of the eight towns they had visited had a sewage disposal system set up by Mr Hillé, a retired Prussian army officer whose instincts for public relations were quite as significant as his sanitary skills. Papillon urged Hillé's methods partly on the success of his existing schemes, partly because he recommended the chemical treatment of sewage in enormous cast-iron tanks, thus avoiding the expense which would be considerable for Colchester of purchasing 50 acres for a sewage farm.[20]

Hillé was therefore engaged to recommend a scheme, the details of which, submitted two months later, largely vindicated those who argued that no national consensus yet existed, least of all among the experts, on the most satisfactory way to dispose of sewage. There was a marked disparity between Denton's and Hillé's calculations, while Hillé's estimates were even higher than Denton's. An outlay of £50,000 for sewers and sewage works seemed likely, and particular doubts were cast, quite rightly, on the £400 a year Hillé would charge for the supply of chemicals, all of which were well known and considerably cheaper on the open market. Moreover, even while the Council had been convincing itself of the superiority of chemical disposal, nearby Halstead, which had adopted Hillé's methods, was pronouncing most unfavourably upon them, while that respected authority, Sir Joseph Bazalgette, builder of the main drainage system of London, was denouncing all chemical systems as costly and unsatisfactory, and proclaiming tidal outfalls – a method feasible at Colchester – as by far the best procedure. Sewage disposal, observed the mayor, on receiving these contradictory proposals, was becoming as complicated as the Eastern Question. Hillé was therefore shelved, and another year of indecision passed. The perplexed Borough Council must have been much reassured by the stern pronouncement of Bawtree Harvey, appearing as a letter in the press, that the current state of national uncertainty on the subject fully justified continued postponement of the sewerage question.[21]

While this may have reassured the Council, it had quite the opposite effect upon the millers, Wilson Marriage and Ezekiel Chopping, especially when it was suggested that one solution would be for the Borough Council to buy up both the mills, dismantle their water courses, and render the River Colne a more efficient agent for sewage disposal. Joining forces, the two men took their case to the Local Government Board. When this produced no more than stiff letters to the Borough Council, they took their case to their solicitors, notifying the Corporation that they would initiate legal proceedings under the Pollution of Rivers Act if something were not done within two months. In part, of course, they were bluffing. The cost to them of a full prosecution was likely to be prohibitive, while experience was already beginning to show that the Pollution of Rivers Act, like so much legislation before it, had too many permissive clauses to guarantee successful prosecutions.[22]

Thus menaced by a blunted Sword of Damocles, the Borough Council groped onward into 1878. If at times they did not take the millers' threat too seriously, or even let it wander from their minds, we should excuse the lapse. Events were closing in on Colchester, on the Conservative Council, on Peter Bruff, on Charlie Hawkins. For 1878 was to have a memorable climax: the years of confrontation had arrived.

Q for the QUARRELS which sometimes occur
  When Tories and Rads in the Council
  confer.
They chiefly arise when the Parties remember
There is such a date as the First of November.

7

1878-1880: Municipal Purchase

Much happened in 1878 to bring together those loose ends left scattered around our previous narrative. Political considerations, never far from the surface in the town's affairs, took on a new intensity at the very moment when the water question was reaching its greatest climax in thirty years. In 1877 Sayers Turner, full of years and secrets, resigned as Town Clerk of Colchester. He was rewarded with the scarlet robes of an alderman, an honour considered not at all inappropriate by his Conservative friends. According to the Liberal newspaper, Turner had stepped down to enable a younger man to prosecute the Conservative cause in the borough with greater vigour now that their forty-year domination of Council affairs was under some threat. While this is not usually regarded as the main function of a chief executive, the Liberals had reasons for their claim. One was Turner's successor. His office passed to the pugnacious Henry Jones, an appointment violently opposed by the Liberal leader, James Wicks. It was not Jones's ability which was questioned; that was well known. Nor was it the controversial circumstances under which he had recently lost his own seat as a Borough Councillor. It was not even his sharp dealing over a recent insurance case that had been widely reported in the press, though Wicks, never one to miss the opportunity, brought this episode up. Henry Jones's main disqualification in Liberal eyes was that he was one of the most active Conservative protagonists in the Colchester district, being, in particular, official Party Agent for North Essex. Clearly the role of Town Clerk as "wire puller in chief" was to be perpetuated. Henry Jones also operated, from behind the Town Hall, one of the largest and most flourishing legal practices in the area, a livelihood he was not required, and did not intend, to forego in offering his services to the Corporation.[1]

In point of fact the new Town Clerk brought to his office great energy, and that sense of high drama which he regularly employed in courts of law. Nor did he lose sight of a bargain when he saw it. One of his first jobs in 1878 was to oversee the dismantling of old St

Runwald's, the little church, possibly a Saxon foundation, which now stood all alone in the High Street. Unused for several years, its last undignified function was to provide support to a public urinal – one aspect of Victorian public health that need not detain us now.[2] The Victorians considered St Runwald's an eyesore, but subsequent generations of Colcestrians have regarded it with peculiar fascination. Little of it was wasted. Its gothic windows went to St Martin's, its communion table to St Nicholas, its font to Little Totham, its chancel arcade to St Albright's, Stanway, and Henry Jones took the rest. The thick walls provided the stone with which he built two large houses on Maldon Road, The Cloisters and St Runwalds, which still stand today. So too do the roads he extended from them, named, appropriately, after successive Conservative Prime Ministers, Beaconsfield and Salisbury Avenues.[3]

More significantly, Henry Jones marked his first year in office by offering the Council a three-fold programme of municipal action. In a lengthy speech he argued that a fresh attempt should be made to widen and deepen the tidal reaches of the Colne; that the still water basin proposed 35 years before should be built; and that the borough should proceed with the purchase of the Gas and Waterworks Companies. In the case of the Gas Company, however, the Town Clerk quickly added, with one eye on its Colchester shareholders, it might be wiser to await the outcome of the experiments now taking place with electric lighting. No such reservations were offered about the Waterworks. The disastrous fire of February had crystallized opinion in the town. Unlike the Gas Company, the Waterworks were not owned and managed by members of the Colchester business community. Peter Bruff of Ipswich was on his own – or rather, almost on his own, and Henry Jones was quick to see the implication of this. Carefully reading Dodd's 1808 Act of incorporation, under whose terms the Waterworks were

SAYERS TURNER (1815-1880), for 28 years Town Clerk of Colchester, was, claimed his obituary, "the genial and unaffected leader of the Conservative Party", whose genius lay not in intellectual attainment but in "knowing how to select the most fitting agents to perform the political work required."

operated, he fixed upon the clause that forbade any person with an interest in the Waterworks from owning more than 20 of the original £100 shares. Now it was widely known that the Waterworks had been purchased in 1851 by Bruff and William Hawkins, whose shares were now held by his widow. If these were the only two shareholders, the terms of the Act of Parliament had clearly been abused for 26 years; Bruff's company was a monopoly and could not support in a court of law its claim of Parliamentary authority for alone supplying Colchester with water.[4]

In point of fact Henry Jones had been peculiarly well placed to know all this from the inside. When Dodd's Company was established in 1808, its Colchester Agent (for it was a London-based Company) was Francis Tillett Abell, mayor, alderman and leading citizen. In the fullness of time his place as Agent was taken by his son, Francis Gibbs Abell, himself a leading attorney in the town. Such an inheritance suggests that the family were shareholders too. In the fullness of yet more time F.G. Abell took into his office and later into his partnership a young law clerk. In between occasional brushes with the police, the young clerk courted and married his employer's daughter. The young law clerk was Henry Jones, and Francis Abell was thus in every sense his father-in-law. Soon after the betrothal negotiations began which led to the sale of the Waterworks to Bruff and Hawkins. It seems improbable that Francis Abell and therefore Henry Jones were not privy to the terms of this transaction. Henry Jones certainly showed detailed knowledge of the old company when he became Town Clerk and may even have been party to the illegalities he now attempted to exploit.[5]   For when the Town Council assembled in the wake of the High Street fire, their new Town Clerk strongly advised them to bring a test case for negligence on the grounds that Dodd's Act of Parliament also committed the Waterworks Company to maintaining a fire engine. The main purpose of this ploy would be to enable Henry Jones to ask some awkward questions in open court. Such belligerence the Council deemed uncalled for, possibly from being lent on in advance by Alderman Hawkins. Meanwhile Henry Jones had already written to F.W. Tindall, solicitor and Secretary of the Waterworks Company:

"Will you let me know for the information of the Town Council the names and residences of the persons who hold shares in the Colchester Waterworks . . . and the number held by each person . . . I want these particulars for the guidance of the Corporation with reference to the desirability of taking the water supply into their own hands".

Tindall's reply was evasive. Henry Jones therefore wrote off for a copy of the latest *Digest of Laws Relating to Public Health,* and tried again:

> "I am in receipt of your favour . . . and beg to observe that
> my enquiry as to the number of shareholders was made in
> order that I might be enabled to inform the local authority
> whether your company was still in existence under the
> Parliamentary restriction contained in the Act limiting the
> number of shares to be held by each person, and if you still
> decline to give me the particulars . . . I shall be compelled
> to assume that . . . the Urban Sanitary Authority may
> consider they have no Company with Parliamentary
> powers to treat with".[6]

No declaration of war could be more clearly stated. For Henry Jones knew from his *Digest* that under the 1875 Public Health Act there were three ways whereby a local authority might operate municipal waterworks. They might purchase an existing company with that company's agreement, or they might turn to the government for powers of compulsory purchase. These however were not easily obtained and would doubtless prove both acrimonious and expensive. Thirdly, an authority might initiate their own works where an existing company was not based on Parliamentary incorporation. Might it now be possible to demonstrate that the Colchester Waterworks Company was not? Indeed, in March, in a long memorandum to the Council, outlining the history of the waterworks, Henry Jones recommended just this.

The time has come to feel sorry for Peter Bruff. For the past six years he had been devoting time, energy and capital to improving the Colchester Waterworks. A new engine house had been built, new pumps had been fitted, new engines and boilers installed. The length of mains had been increased by 50% and, although some were as narrow as 1.5 inches diameter, he could claim to be serving virtually all the built-up area of the town. The number of customers and weekly output of water had doubled and plans were afoot to complete a second artesian bore beside the original one at the foot of Balkerne Hill. He had even laboured for the past two years to bring the Borough Sanitary Committee to agreement over a comprehensive fire-fighting procedure. Perhaps even to his own surprise, these exertions and the addition of new customers had actually rendered the company a going concern, realising, at last, some profit on its operations. Moreover, having just received £15,000 for his land and Deed of Covenant at Clacton, he was far better placed than he had ever been before to finance further capital development. Now all this was to be threatened by awkward questions in a court of law.[7]

It is unlikely that so experienced and shrewd a man as Bruff had ever been ignorant of his failure to comply with his Act of incorporation.

But only in the last few years, since the talk of municipal purchase, had this really mattered. Since then there is evidence that he had tried to adjust the situation. For example, many of his shares had been moved sideways to his sons and to his close Ipswich colleague, the solicitor, George Josselyn. Similarly some of Mrs Hawkins's holdings seem to have been transferred to her brother-in-law, Colonel Hawkins. Then there was the disturbing obligation of accounting for some 25 Annual General Meetings, notices of which should have appeared in both the Colchester and London press. This would explain an item solemnly printed in the *Essex Standard* as early as August 1876, describing the "Annual General Meeting of the Waterworks Company", detailing its impressive progress in plant and extensions, and noting, as was customary at such events, that the retiring Director (note the singular) was duly re-elected. Was this Peter Bruff or Mrs Hawkins, and, presuming that the meeting even took place, were there more than three persons present? Now in the spring of 1878 Peter Bruff could well imagine the sort of mileage this could all afford to Henry Jones and his familiar barn-storming courtroom style. Of course there was hope that Bruff's Conservative friends on the Borough Council would sidetrack their aggressive Town Clerk, but the Conservative majority was now quite slender and might not last another year.[8]

Peter Bruff therefore fell back upon the good contacts and long experience of Parliamentary procedure he had gained while planning, opposing, undermining and subsequently disentangling railway projects. A man who had seen at first hand the rise and fall of George Hudson should not be underestimated. Besides, he had had quite recent practice.

Only six months previously, Bruff's Walton-on-the-Naze Gas and Water Company had come to the end of a seven-year agreement with the Walton Commissioners for supplying gas and water to the town. The Commissioners, of whom Bruff of course was one, dissatisfied with both commodities in terms of price and quality, had prevaricated over renewing the seven-year agreement and entered into discussion over the possibility of buying the Waterworks from Bruff. One of the most tenacious defenders of the 'rights' of the Commissioners was their Clerk and legal advisor, Frederick Philbrick, who now owned property in the town. Faced with such doughty opposition, Bruff stalled. Then, in mid-November, with negotiations still in progress, on the last possible occasion in the Parliamentary calendar, he applied for a Provisional Order to give his company statutory powers to provide gas and water to the town. Caught by surprise, the indignant Commissioners resolved to oppose this move. Philbrick, that stern opponent of bad smells and arrogant officials, even opposed the Order in his private capacity as a ratepayer on the grounds that the fumes and presence of the Gasworks were a permanent offence to his house nearby. The Public Enquiry in the following March, conducted while

Henry Jones was busy writing threatening letters, fully upheld Bruff's application. With only minor amendments, the Board of Trade allowed his incorporation to proceed.[9]

Without apparently noting these events, Henry Jones continued writing letters, this time to Peter Bruff:

> "In the hope that it may not be necessary for the Urban Sanitary Authority to avail themselves of any advantage which they believe is open to them with regards to the Colchester Waterworks, I am directed to ask whether you are disposed to sell the same to the Colchester Urban Sanitary Authority . . ."

Some might call this blackmail. It was certainly neither conciliatory nor diplomatic. Bruff stalled. Henry Jones wrote again. Bruff replied that he did not wish to sell, but left the door open for negotiations which, informally, began. In September the Town Clerk advised the Council to take out a Provisional Order. They set up a Committee. In November, on the afternoon of the last possible day that session for submitting such a measure, Bruff and Josselyn introduced a private Bill to Parliament that would greatly increase the power of the Colchester Waterworks Company, eliminate their vulnerability under the 1808 Act, legalise everything they had done since 1851, establish their capital value as £35,000 (it was currently £15,000) and transform their negotiating position in the event of an attempted compulsory purchase by the Corporation. It was a carbon copy of their successful tactics at Walton the year before. Indeed it is remarkable that in all the events that followed, the comparison was not once made at Colchester.[10]

The Borough Council had scarcely had time to absorb the implications of Bruff's move when they received another blow. In January the case of Marriage and Chopping v. the Corporation of Colchester came before the County Court. Obviously the millers had not been bluffing after all, or rather they had taken their bluff a stage further. Negotiations therefore took place and the millers agreed in court to let their prosecution stand over for two more years under the terms of the Pollution of Rivers Act, on the clear undertaking that the Corporation would begin forthwith to install a new and proper sewerage system. The Corporation also, of course, met the millers' costs. These however were minimal beside the major expenditure to which the town would now be committed.[11]

This fact must have overshadowed the Public Meeting of the town which the Corporation now called to seek support for opposition to Bruff's new Waterworks Bill. Moreover the presence of Henry Jones as chief proponent of the Borough's case inevitably recalled his action as a private citizen only three years before in leading the disastrous opposition to the Gas Improvement Bill. Shrewdly anticipating the likely public response and probably with the consent of his Tory colleagues, Henry Jones made a dramatic visit to Ipswich 48 hours before the Public Meeting to effect some sort of deal with Peter Bruff. The package with which he breathlessly returned was then dramatically unwrapped and steamrollered upon a not unwilling, though rather shell-shocked, audience. There was to be a compromise. Bruff would consent to sell the Waterworks to the Corporation, if they agreed to withdraw their opposition to his Bill, and join him in submitting a joint Bill to Parliament.

This offer seemed attractive, but it begged the important questions of what the joint Bill would say and how much the Waterworks would cost. Moreover the boot was now upon the other foot. The longer Bruff stalled, the further his present Bill would progress towards the statute book, forcing Colchester to make the expensive decision either to oppose his Bill or, worse still, not to oppose it. The new relationship was sharply underlined by endless visits to Ipswich of the Colchester negotiating team made up essentially of Alderman Papillon, Councillor Wicks and Henry Jones. Using a formula recommended in the 1875 Public Health Act, they proposed a purchase price based on the average earnings of the Waterworks for five years up to June 1878 multiplied by a 25-year period. Bruff and Josselyn refused, insisting instead on the current year's earnings as the basis for negotiation. Two months' haggling followed before the Colchester team capitulated. Bruff had got his way and both sides settled down to appoint their arbitrators.

In practice the Borough Council faced a *fait accompli*. Lacking the will to oppose Bruff in January, they had to accept the best terms their negotiators could get. And yet, as one Liberal Councillor protested, they were effectively signing a blank cheque. Not only were they agreeing to purchase on the basis of the financial year to June 1879 which had not even finished yet, but the Waterworks Company, like the Gas Company before them, had refused to release any figures of their operation. Everyone knew that Bruff was opposed to a purchase based on a five-year average because within that period there were doubts whether the Waterworks had made a profit at all. During the current year, however, matters could no doubt be manipulated to produce a handsome profit. Yet the Corporation did not have the slightest indication of what that profit was.[12]

This was in fact not quite the situation. For Josselyn had clearly dropped broad hints to Henry Jones, hints so broad that the Town Clerk was able to confidently advise the Council to apply to the Local Government Board for a loan of £60,000, in the belief that the Waterworks would cost between £50,000 and £60,000. It therefore came as a severe shock to the assembled Councillors, though not perhaps to us, when in December the arbitrators produced a final award of approximately £82,000, some £20,000 more than anyone had expected and £47,000 more than the value placed on the Company in Bruff's original Bill; a value which, incidently, Henry Jones had denounced as excessive at the Public Meeting in the town. This handsome windfall Bruff presumably divided with Josselyn and Mrs Hawkins, though one cannot help but speculate upon the peculiar role played in these events by Charles Henry Hawkins. As Chairman of the Essex and Suffolk Fire Office, confidant of Bruff and brother-in-law of Mrs Hawkins, it is difficult to believe that he was as uninformed about the proceedings of the Waterworks Company as he asserted he was on every possible public occasion. Yet his was the only voice consistently to urge that the Council could not run the Waterworks as well as the existing Company. Nor did he disguise his dislike of Henry Jones. Together with Sayers Turner and Alderman Smythies (Mrs Hawkins's brother) he argued and voted against municipal purchase, but when the Liberal Councillor made his 'blank cheque' speech, Alderman Hawkins was quick to insist that the terms negotiated at Ipswich were "good terms for the Corporation".[13]

All these byzantine proceedings were rendered more poignant by the peculiar state of borough politics at this time. Ever since the Municipal Corporation Act of 1835, Colchester's borough elections had been the object of party strife. Initially the Liberals had won control, made their defeated candidates aldermen, and thrown out the existing Tory officials. Liberal joy however was shortlived. Within two years they too were overthrown and all the jobs and perquisites changed hands. There followed in their own words "42 Years of Tory Tyranny", during which the Liberals never secured a majority on the Council, while the office of mayor was largely confined to an exclusive band of Conservative aldermen, a monopoly unparralleled in Eastern England. Major Bishop was mayor seven times, Henry Wolton six. Even Dr Williams held the post for four years. The Liberals had really given up when James Wicks came of age.[14]

From the moment he first appeared at a public meeting, standing on his chair and waving his arms, James Wicks was seldom out of the news. A man of intemperate disposition and unrepentant Radical enthusiasm, his capacity for exciting controversy was remarkable even in a politician. To the evident embarrassment of some of his own party, under the banner "Wicks, the People's candidate", all-out war was declared on "The Tory clique". One of the casualties in this onslaught was the respected figure of John Bawtree Harvey, who had increasingly condemned, though reluctantly practised, the pursuit of party in municipal affairs. He had in consequence run the danger of becoming the Conservatives' favourite Liberal. It takes one to know one, and his personal triumph over the Gas Company's Bill drew from Charles Henry Hawkins, his opposite number on the Conservative side, a barbed but clear recognition of a worthy opponent:

The apotheosis of JAMES WICKS, Radical belligerent, seen here in 1896 in his official photograph as mayor of Colchester, an honour he had in fact refused on several previous occasions.

"They all knew of Mr Harvey's business qualities, and
admired his cool, calculative ability".

No Conservative would have said that of James Wicks and the
Conservatives were willing to leave Harvey's Council seat uncontested,
so long as he did not seriously rock the municipal boat. This moral
bribery restricted the Liberal's new offensive and in 1872, in
circumstances that were never openly explained, Harvey declined to
stand for re-election, the paper he had once edited declaring, rather
improbably, that he was now too old for municipal affairs. The net
consequence of the contested elections that followed was the
replacement of Bawtree Harvey by James Wicks.[15]

The People's Candidate had also been elected a member of the
Board of Guardians. Here he discovered quite by accident that the
Clerk, a Tory alderman and ex-mayor, was regularly feasting the
workhouse master and his cronies from public money earmarked for
the poor, whose own strictly controlled diet had proved so beneficial
to the neighbouring pigs. James Wicks was not one to squander such
unexpected godsends from the other side. The erstwhile dull meetings
of the Guardians were soon enlivened by an "Anti-Lunch" party, noted
for their abuse of English syntax and ruthless search for further
skeletons in the workhouse cupboard. Eventually it was shown that the
quantity of brandy purchased for the workhouse sick greatly exceeded
their collective medical requirements. The workhouse master and his
wife left suddenly – and without a reference. The Liberal cause was
looking up.[16]

All this brings us to 1879 and the purchase of the Waterworks from
Bruff. This was conducted on a strict bi-partisan basis under a
Conservative mayor, Thomas Moy, one of East Anglia's leading coal
merchants, who from his offices at the Hythe controlled a chain of
large coal yards the length and breadth of the Great Eastern Railway.
Then in November 1879, a month before the Waterworks arbitration
was announced, the Liberals won five Council seats, and at last secured
political power. The first Liberal mayor for 42 years was robed and
James Wicks was king of Colchester. At times he rather behaved like
it. In January, at a Council meeting for which no agenda was supplied,
leading Conservative officials were systematically disposed of. The
most significant was Henry Jones. He and James Wicks were old
enemies. Twelve years before, Henry Jones had publicly and ruthlessly
humiliated Wicks at a Parliamentary Enquiry held to consider a
petition Wicks had sponsored to unseat one of Colchester's
Conservative M.P.s for electoral corruption. Now Henry Jones was to
be served in kind. Partly with the case of Sayers Turner and the Gas
Company in mind, but also undoubtedly to get rid of Henry Jones, the
Liberals announced that the Town Clerk was to receive a cut in salary
and to be forbidden a private practice of his own. For Henry Jones this

was a choice between suicide and public execution. He chose the former and resigned.[17]

Henry Jones was replaced, almost unbelievably, by Mr Frederick Philbrick, the Liberal ex-Town Clerk, who 42 years before had been ousted by the Conservatives. It was a foolish move. Philbrick was now an old man, over 70, distinctly deaf, much given to petulance and whining, and hardly fitting his alleged qualification of political neutrality. The Liberals, having posed for so long as the "purity party", were now clearly tarred with the same brush as their opponents. Philbrick had in fact already revealed the level of his statesmanship by writing to the Council at their first meeting after the November elections, requesting that a vote of thanks, verbally agreed at his dismissal 42 years before, should now be authenticated in the surviving minutes. Then there was the problem, shrewdly brought out by Alderman Papillon, that Mr Philbrick was still Clerk to the Tendring Hundred Railway Company. Was this not forbidden under the terms of his new contract? It was – and Philbrick got into a bigger mess trying to explain his position. Indeed only Fred Philbrick was capable of the comic opera that followed. Sternly refusing to resign the post in Council, he promptly did so a week later at a meeting of the Railway Board because, he claimed, they disregarded his advice. One might well wonder whether this was the man to replace the astute and pugnacious Henry Jones in steering the town through the deep waters of the Water Bill.

Also dismissed on this Day of the Long Knives was Joseph Hope, Borough Surveyor, whose services to the town stretched back over 35 years. He was replaced by his young deputy, Charles Clegg, who had just completed the designs for a do-it-ourselves sewerage system for the town: the promised response to the Marriage/Chopping County Court agreement. Clegg's pedigree was impressive. Son of a gifted engineer, his grandfather, also an engineer, had designed the world's first effective gas meter. The young man's technical qualifications were also good and his plans for new outfall sewage mains had been much praised by the Chief Engineer to the Local Government Board, Sir Robert Rawlinson, who had known Clegg's family well. But did Charles Clegg's precocious skills offset his inexperience?[18]

Meanwhile the Conservatives on the Council, smarting from these defeats, turned for compensation to revenge – some might call it wrecking. Alderman Papillon took offence when his name was omitted, apparently in innocence, from membership of the Sanitary Committee. He therefore resigned from all the Council Committees he was on. Why not resign as alderman as well, suggested James Wicks. Thomas Moy, not a poor man, stuck out for a grossly inflated price for a piece of Hythe meadowland he owned that was needed for the new sewage works. Quite unabashed, Henry Jones, who was not once consulted by Philbrick about the Waterworks, submitted a bill for £515 to the town for his professional charges in concluding the transaction. The Council, forced to read the small print (which Henry Jones had written) reluctantly paid up, but James Wicks made sure that a Liberal newspaper printed every item of the bill. Such unprofessional conduct brought political controversy to fresh heights, mirroring in the Council Chamber the current antics of those Parliamentary giants, Gladstone and Disraeli, then at the peak of their fury.[19]

In this relaxed atmosphere, Fred Philbrick directed his forensic skills to his *"damnosa hereditas"*, the purchase of the Waterworks. Confident that more concessions could be wrung from Bruff and Josselyn and concerned that the clauses of the joint Bill had been less than closely considered, he seized upon the technicality that the mayor had used the wrong borough seal in confirming the formal agreement, practically the last deed of Henry Jones's brief reign as Town Clerk. On these tenuous grounds Philbrick opened up the whole contract once more. Turning to his eldest son, a London Q.C., whose legal opinions cost the Borough 50 guineas a time, he tried to improve the Council's terms under the agreement. He had little success, but as a result it was October 1880 before the purchase was completed, by which time the original sum awarded to Bruff of £81,218 had grown by £5,111 accumulated interest. In fairness to Philbrick it should be said that the chief cause of delay was the continued failure of Bruff and Josselyn to produce any abstract of title to the Waterworks. Unfortunately the prolonged scutiny which this engendered did not extend to the removal of a clause by Henry Jones which would have permitted the Borough to raise the purchase money in the form of a mortgage on the Waterworks, the value of which, as we have seen, was now considerable. Henry Jones later maintained that the clause had been removed at the bidding of the Chairman of the Parliamentary Committee to consider such Bills, but its loss was to cause further complications.[20]

With Alderman Papillon no longer available, James Wicks assumed the chairmanship of the Waterworks Committee. By any standards this was a questionable inheritance too. The Borough had appointed as their arbitrator Edward Easton, an experienced engineer who had been involved in the now famous purchase of their Waterworks by Birmingham, whose guiding spirit, Joseph Chamberlain, was now a leading Liberal politician. The subsequent profitability of the Birmingham scheme was one James Wicks was fond of quoting. At the same time as his appointment, Easton was also commissioned to supply the Council with a report on the improvements necessary to the Waterworks for the Council to meet their obligations under current legislation. Two thoughts were uppermost in this request: the need for an instant and large provision of water in the event of fire and the town's future ability to maintain a constant supply of water under pressure to all parts of the borough.

Easton's report underlined the chief deficiency of Bruff's works: by pumping direct into the mains it was necessary to zone the town and serve each part in turn, thus providing only an intermittent supply. At night, when the engines were not running, there was, as we have seen in the case of fires, no water under pressure at all. Easton therefore proposed a large reservoir that would hold 1,000,000 gallons, the likely daily supply needed in the town before long. This could be sited near the Mile End Road on land already owned by the Borough, approximately where Defoe Crescent stands today. At 166 feet above sea level this would be sufficient elevation to serve the town. The valuable piece of land which housed the reservoir inside the Balkerne Gate could then be sold. To provide the increased supply that would be needed, a new bore should be made at the Balkerne Works, new premises constructed and new engines installed. The total cost would be £11,500.[21]

Was this a viable scheme? Modern engineers consider that the Mile End reservoir would in practice have lacked the height to provide the pressure to gravity feed water to the upper floors of the highest parts of the inhabited town. In the light of his subsequent decisions it seems probable that Charles Clegg shared this view, but it is interesting to note that a Mile End reservoir was again proposed in 1892 and 1906. It is also curious to note that the matter was never discussed by the Waterworks Committee. Nor was a reason ever given for thus rejecting Easton's scheme. Why? Two explanations suggest themselves. Firstly, Easton very soon fell out with the Corporation. Henry Jones claimed that this was because of Philbrick's legal duplicity over the matter of the mayor's seal. It might equally have been the reluctance of the Liberal majority to deal with a man who had supported an arbitration award of £82,000. The second possible reason for the rejection of Easton's scheme was Charles Clegg. The youthful Borough Surveyor appears to have advised the chairman of the Waterworks Committee, deeply worried as he and his colleagues were about expenditure, that a do-it-ourselves scheme, based on the old idea of a water-tower, would be cheaper than £11,500. Time was to show how true this was.[22]

In any event Easton's departure from the scene had one unfortunate result. Casting around for means to pay for the Waterworks, the Council had advertised for a loan of £100,000 in £100 debentures at 4% interest, repaid at 60 years. Some £67,000 was offered, the lion's share (£50,000) by Edward Easton, either for himself or for an influential contact. With Easton's departure the offer disappeared too and the Council, prevented by their own Act from raising a mortgage on the Waterworks, had to revert to the Local Government Board whose interest rate (4.5%) was higher and whose period of repayment (50 years) was shorter. Combined, these factors would inevitably lead to larger current repayments. So far, of course, on the strength of a broad hint, the Council had secured approval for a £60,000 loan, by far the largest in the borough's history, believing this to be adequate to buy the Waterworks. Now it was not. Approval therefore had to be sought to raise a further £23,500 to cover the original purchase price. (This did not of course include the £5,111 interest that had now accrued). By a splendid effrontery the entire £23,000 loan came from separate contributions by the following individuals: Peter Bruff, Peter Bruff's son, George Josselyn, George Josselyn's son, William Tindall, late Secretary to the Waterworks, and Colonel Septimus Hawkins, brother of Charles Henry Hawkins. It is difficult not to see in this, suitably laundered, the anticipated profits of the Waterworks' sale. For thanks to Fred Philbrick's bold attempts at renegotiation, the final payment for the Waterworks actually took place after these indentures had been confirmed. It is thus not too much of an over-simplification to say that for 4.5% Peter Bruff lent Colchester the money with which to buy the Waterworks from him, the sort of transaction of which George Hudson would have been proud. Even with this assistance, the Corporation was in such dire straits for money and so overdrawn at the bank, they they asked for, and were magnanimously granted by Bruff, permission to postpone payment of the final £1,000 interest for a further eight months.[23]

Thus did the Corporation of Colchester acquire its Waterworks. On a brisk morning in October 1880 a formal ceremony took place at the Company's premises at the foot of Balkerne Hill. Peter Bruff solemnly lined up the five employees to tell them that the Corporation was now their master whom they should in future all obey. Thus reprogrammed the men returned to their tasks, bickering among themselves over their profitable side-lines of growing watercress and goldfish in the overflow reservoir beside the pumping house.[24] Colchester now owned the Waterworks; what would it make of them?

I stands for INTEREST, formerly paid
  At a Liberal rate, by the Liberal Brigade ;
Their Charge it was wild, and the ratepayers
  wondered,
Until it was evident someone had blundered.

8

1880-1885: Municipal Tribulations

The birth of a new era is often a disappointment. Only with hindsight does it appear significant, let alone auspicious. The passing of the Waterworks into public ownership meant that henceforward the provision of a service to the public was to be of more importance than the realisation of a profit. At least, that was the theory of the case against Peter Bruff. Yet such was the disposition of Victorian attitudes and the age-old suspicion of public spending, that the beleaguered Borough Council, or should we say its Liberal majority, were haunted during the next decade by their own claims that the Waterworks should be, indeed would be, a profitable undertaking. The combined requirements of political survival and 19th-century economics put them forever on the defensive. Whatever statistics they might with justice parade as evidence of more water pumped to more people for a longer period, these could so readily be dismissed by the jibes that the Council was expending large sums of money and that the water rates had gone up. There was also at a less political level a psychological response more familiar to the 20th century. As any public servant has discovered in our anonymous, collectivist world, there is a naive and touching assumption that anything promoted in the public name should be at once gratuitous and without flaw. The professional grumblers of Victorian Colchester, faced with the failure of municipal waterpipes, registered a sharper sense of outrage than if the culprit had been Peter Bruff. The Liberal predicament is epitomised by the fact that the furore that was to cause their political discomfort was brought about by their efforts to *improve* the services of the Waterworks, an intent that was at once both worthy and not without an element of success.[1]

With Easton's money gone and Easton's scheme abandoned (fees £139), the Waterworks Committee was now dependent upon Charles Clegg. Appointed as Engineer to the Waterworks, his first report exuded confidence:

"I see no absolute or immediate reason to fear that the
works as at present are inadequate to furnish the necessary
water supply . . ."

Some time afterwards, for reasons that will soon become apparent, an
amused Councillor has put a pencilled exclamation mark against this
entry in the minute book. For the moment however the greatest
urgency was to secure yet another loan from the Local Government
Board. This was necessary not only to pay Bruff's remaining £1,000
interest, but to help finance the drilling of a second artesian well at the
Waterworks, a measure which Peter Bruff had long contemplated and
Easton had recommended in his report. This time the Council asked
for £2,500, but with ominous precision they were held down to the
exact sum of £2,412. It was the Borough's misfortune that this second
drilling was not to be as fruitful as the first memorable bore of 1852.
But they did not know this yet and on both Easton's and Clegg's advice
the Waterworks Committee terminated the leases on the Sheepen
Spring and the spring at Osborne's Brewery which Bruff had been
using as an auxiliary supply for the east end of the town.[2]
    With the new bore apparently functioning successfully, in August
1881 the Waterworks Committee was ready to make a momentous
decision. Their new Engineer submitted plans and estimates for a
water-tower on Balkerne Hill holding 220,000 gallons and costing
£6,700. It was a very full meeting and there was lengthy discussion, but
at no stage was the proposal for a water-tower seriously challenged. In
a sense an idea already 30 years old had put down strong roots. After
all, scale drawings had existed since 1866.
    Yet it might easily have been otherwise. Setting aside Easton's
reservoir proposals, the idea of meeting all Colchester's needs from a
single water-tower had had some distinguished opponents. One was
Peter Bruff. His expansion of the Waterworks during the late 1870s
had involved considerable investment, but no Balkerne water-tower
had been built. Rather Bruff had favoured several towers. One already
functioned on Lexden Road, another was at Osborne's Brewery, and
land to hold a third, purchased by Bruff in the New Town area, had
already been sold off by a Waterworks Committee facing, in every
sense, serious liquidity problems. Another water-tower doubter had
been John Bawtree Harvey. When the water-tower question was
seriously looked into following the 1873 fire, Harvey unequivocally
concluded that:

"with only one tower they should not be able to get a
constant supply for private consumers throughout the
whole town. For instance, they could not from a tower on
Balkerne Hill constantly supply the Hythe and East Hill –

there would be no difficulty as to water, but the pressure
on the pipes would be too great"

Although some eight years later he now gave the idea his guarded
support, evidence was soon to show the soundness of his earlier
caution: much trenching for new water pipes lay ahead.

For the moment, however, the water-tower had become a foregone
conclusion. The same could not be said about the means to pay for
it and it was this that largely occupied discussion on that August
evening. The Borough Treasurer pointed out that despite a recent
reassessment of the water rate (i.e. an increase), their present income
was not sufficient to cover the additional repayments and interest on
a loan that would have to be large enough to finance not only a water-
tower, but a rising main to bring the water from the new well at the
foot of Balkerne Hill. The only
hope of balancing the books lay
in the additional income likely
to arise from the £1,000 they
had just spent on renewing and
extending the mains in the fast-
developing east end of Colchester. Despite the Borough
Treasurer's optimism, this was a
tenuous basis on which to
proceed. Moreover the new
loan, like its predecessors,
would have to be set against the
General District Rate as a security and therein lay a further
problem.[3]

The area covered by the ancient borough of Colchester is
extraordinarily large: nearly 16
square miles in fact. Even today
most of the built-up area of the
town still lies within these
limits. Such size is apparently
the product of remarkable
historical continuity, loudly proclaimed on all approach roads to
the town. "Welcome to Colchester, Britain's Oldest Recorded Town", the placards say.
This carefully worded assertion
is based on the fact that before
the Roman Conquest the settle-

*PHILIP OXENDEN PAPILLON M.P.
(1826-1899), vulgarly known as POP, did
not easily fit the Radical classification of
The Idle Rich. Educated by Dr. Arnold at
Rugby and a qualified barrister, he assi-
duously followed the callings of Lord of the
Manor, Justice of the Peace and Borough
Alderman - until, that is, the Liberals
gained supremacy.*

ment then called Camulodunum served as the defended headquarters of Cunobelin, popularly known as Cymbeline, whom the Romans called King of the Britons. With adjustments to the north and east, this large defended area formed, a thousand years later, the basis of the medieval borough.[4] Consequently in the 19th century the administrative area of Colchester included totally rural communities like Mile End or self-contained villages like Lexden over two miles from the town centre. Even the sweeping promises of Dodd's Waterworks Act did not extend to these parishes. However the joint Bill of 1880 did, and discussion that August evening was overshadowed by the consequences. Realising the increased rate burden they might face, the rural parishes had protested, pointing out that the Public Health Act of 1875 empowered local authorities to charge rural areas a lower rate, if they so decided. What gave the matter a political edge was the fact that most of the rural parishes were owned by a handful of landowners. Leading the attack upon the Borough Council was the largest resident landlord of all, the Lord of the Manor of Lexden, Alderman Papillon.

Papillon did his homework well. Colchester's area relative to its population was, he claimed, the second largest of any borough in England. Nine-tenths of it was wholly rural and largely detached from the urban parishes. To meet just such a situation the exemption clauses had been added to the Public Health Act.[5] The Liberals however were swift with a counter argument, recognising in Alderman Papillon the living embodiment of that Radical bogy, the landed classes, whom their hero, Joseph Chamberlain, was soon to label

> "an oligarchy which is a mere accident of birth . . . who toil not neither do they spin, whose fortunes . . . originated in grants made . . . for the services which courtiers rendered kings, and have since grown and increased, while they have slept, by levying an increased share on all that other men have done by toil . . ."[6]

Alderman Papillon and his friends, protested a Liberal Councillor, had made considerable untaxed fortunes from selling land on the outskirts of the town, like the Lord's Land Estate, for housing development. Only the presence of Colchester made this land so valuable. Yet here were these wealthy men refusing to pay rates on the same terms as others.

Papillon however had a point. 'Rural' Colchester, which contributed one third of the General District Rate, received no services whatsoever from the municipally-owned waterworks, nor were they likely to benefit from the expensive new sewers and sewage works about to be provided for the town. Yet these two facilities were likely to involve combined loans of £140,000 which, set against the District Rate, would leave a burden of interest and repayments for 50 years to come. Small

wonder therefore that on that August evening Fred Philbrick warned
the Waterworks Committee that further loans might lead to trouble.
Far better, he advised, to seek enlarged powers from Parliament than
go once more to the Local Government Board for a loan. Philbrick's
advice however was not taken, but it may explain the unwise decision
that was eventually arrived at to reduce the size of the new loan from
£12,000 to £10,000.

And so the August meeting of the Waterworks Committee
concluded, taking as it did the unusual step of passing, unanimously,
a long and rather wordy motion. It was proposed, appropriately, by
John Bawtree Harvey, once more restored to the Borough Council:

> "... in the opinion of the meeting, the requirements of the
> town in the matter of water supply can only be met by a
> Water Tower and Tank of sufficient capacity to ensure, by
> means of the existing well and pumps, a constant supply
> to consumers and provision of adequate storage for
> extinction of fire".

This was a very carefully phrased motion, as anything proposed by
Harvey invariably was, and it provided the basis on which the full
Council approved the building of the water-tower. Much talk was
made by Wicks, the Chairman, of the great blessings that would follow
the introduction of a constant supply, a desideratum which in effect
had been on the agenda since 1847. But as yet no lay member of the
Committee, and possibly not even Clegg himself, had seriously
calculated whether the proposed tower would really meet this
promised goal "by means of the existing well and pumps".[7]

The motion carried, 1882 proved a busy year. Tenders were sought
for the new tower and tank and it was the subject of local gratification
that in open competition both contracts went to local firms. The tank
and ironwork were to be supplied by Arthur Mumford of the Culver
Street Ironworks and the brick tower was built by Henry Everett and
Son of Hythe Hill, a firm still active one hundred years later. What was
less encouraging was that both their estimates, although the lowest
tendered, were higher than Clegg had budgeted for.[8] All this caused
great anxiety to the Waterworks Committee and to its energetic
Chairman, James Wicks. Quite apart from his own business as a retail
wine and spirit merchant, his position as effectively the leader of the
Liberal majority on the Council committed him to Council activity
almost every night of the week. He was also, you will recall, a
prominent member of the Guardians, and was rarely absent from any
public meeting in the town. Despite this he pursued his position as
Chairman of the Committee with great zest. Beyond its regular
meetings the Committee had also set up two small Sub-Committees
where vital decisions were often made at meetings attended by only

two or three people. Wicks and Clegg alone were rarely absent. The whole Waterworks affair which had begun as a corporate venture was becoming, under political pressure and the Chairman's enthusiasm, "Wicks's job".[9]

This was not always popular, even with his fellow Liberals. In August with the footings for the new tower complete, Wicks planned a little ceremony at which he would lay an official foundation stone. A leading Liberal objected to this civic event being organised by the Waterworks Committee rather than the Borough Council. Wicks therefore cancelled it. Meanwhile the Waterworks Committee, equally concerned by the image their Chairman was projecting, ruled at their next meeting that reports to the main Council should in future not be made by the Chairman but by two other members and the Town Clerk. Wicks however was not to be done out of his ceremony, and in October a somewhat bizarre occasion took place. By now the water-tower had reached 30 feet in height. Colchester's two M.P.s (both Liberals) and members of the Corporation were therefore invited to ascend a dangerous looking ladder to a little platform to lay "the Corporation Bricks". Thence they descended to be feasted with champagne and biscuits provided by James Wicks, who also presented half a crown to each of Everett's workmen. The event was thinly attended. Only 11 out of the 24 Council members joined Everett, Wicks and the two M.P.s. More significantly only two of them were Conservatives. Fortunately the event was immortalised, their collective initials being engraved on 15 commemorative bricks, still visible on the south-west corner of the tower. In the absence of accurate records, these provide our only evidence for the speed at which building progressed.[10]

Such public diversions should not however detract from the shopkeeper thoroughness with which the affairs of the Waterworks were now conducted. Though the pounds were increasingly getting out of control, the pence were sternly harvested. A thorough check of all water consumers in the town had revealed a minor industry in illegal pipe-tapping, either from a neighbour's or the public mains. James Wicks soon put a stop to such "pilfering", effecting an annual saving of £50. Other consumers were found to be using water for forbidden extravagances like baths or a second water closet. Posters and handbills were issued proscribing such illegalities. The five Waterworks' employees were denied their profitable side-line in selling water-cress and the franchise was put out to competitive tender. Two thousand goldfish were sold for £8 and water was delivered by rail in special tanks to Walton-on-the-Naze, still vainly awaiting Peter Bruff's promised improved supply.

More signifcantly, new water mains were laid in Colchester and old ones replaced. A revised assessment of the water rate was completed that was both fair and rational. Above all, there was a flood of applications from new customers with which the harrassed borough officials could barely cope. By mid 1883, the number of houses served by the company had risen from 3,357 to 4,520, an increase of 34% since purchase was completed. Clearly, this represented some sort of popular endorsement of public ownership.[11] Throughout these months James Wicks exuded confidence, even exhilaration, but how far this was a mere response to the exercise of power and how far it was a brave front in face of mounting problems is another question. For problems were proliferating. The water-tower was taking longer to complete, costing more than predicted and, worst of all, might not fulfil its main purpose.

Firstly there was the tank. Clegg's original design was circular and made from wrought iron. This was rejected out of hand by Clegg's mentor, Sir Robert Rawlinson, in favour of a cast iron, square tank. Such specifications were really beyond the technology of the Culver Street Iron Works, and Arthur Mumford promptly sub-contracted with a firm in Newcastle. Secondly, late in the day, Clegg decided that the tower should be eleven feet higher, bringing the base of the tank to about 190 feet above sea level, clear evidence both of Clegg's appreciation of the need for adequate elevation as well as the sketchiness of his earlier calculations. This of course involved more bricks. Before long it was being claimed that the tower was the second largest of its kind in England – an appropriate acquisition for the second largest borough. Small wonder that its final cost was over £11,000 compared to Clegg's estimate of £6,700. The Waterworks Committee was now in such financial straits that a bank overdraft was needed to pay the final instalments to Mumfords and Everetts. This however did not prevent a prolonged haggle over whether Everetts should pay for the water they had used in the construction work.

The worst news of all came at a meeting of the Waterworks Committee in May 1883, the tower by now being almost complete. The minutes record:

> The Chairman (Wicks) interrogated the Engineer (Clegg) as to whether a constant supply so as to do away with house storage cisterns would be possible with the new tank. The Engineer conceded . . . that no town supplied by means of a tower could have an absolute constant supply unless the tank held a day's consumption. The new tank would hold six hours' supply and therefore it would be necessary to cut off certain parts of the Borough during day time as under the present system".[12]

This information must have come as a shattering blow to James Wicks. Quite apart from the cash crisis it had created, the 'water question' had also become a vital political issue. In part Wicks was to blame. His somewhat royal style, coupled with his outspoken claims, left him a hostage if his promises were not met or if the Engineer should so disastrously miscalculate.

One man had early spotted the party advantage of all this. Charles Henry Hawkins, friend of Bruff and Conservative godfather, whose family had confidently invested in the new concern, was now vindicated in his claim that the Borough could not run the Waterworks as cheaply as the old Company had. The Conservatives, who had initially expected that their loss of municipal control would last for many years, began to see clear daylight in the tunnel. Alderman Hawkins however was not to share that triumph. For 42 years no Liberal alderman had been elected. Now there were to be no Conservative ones. Hustled from his aldermanic chair and the Council seat he had held for 36 years, the shock to Hawkins's system was so great that he fell seriously ill and was not seen in Colchester again for five years.[13] The water question was hotting up. It needed only a spark or slogan to give it popular appeal.

That slogan was now provided by the Rector of St Mary's-at-the-Walls, the Rural Dean, that practised exhumer of corpses, the Rev. Canon Irvine. Failing to read the statutory notices on his own church door, it came as a nasty shock to him to discover that the second largest water-tower in England was to be built 16 feet from the back of his rectory; that it would carry, 85 feet above his head, a cast iron tank designed to hold, according to the latest estimate, 230,000 gallons of water.

The REV. JOHN IRVINE exuding disapproval at the thought of 1,000 tons of water suspended 85 feet above his rectory garden.

Irvine was an outspoken man and like James Wicks welcomed a good argument, usually prefacing his remarks by the expression, "Pardon me". His considerable sense of personal dignity reflected a cultivated background. Although still mourning the death of his brother, bitten by a cheetah while sporting with the Maharajah of Vizianagram, Irvine was ready if necessary to launch the Ninth Crusade in order to forestall this hideous water-tower. He opened with a proposal. Through the good offices of his friend, the Headmaster, Irvine offered the Waterworks Committee an alternative site on land owned by the Grammar School. Advised by Fred Philbrick, the Committee turned this down, but they did agree to move the tower to the eastern limit of the corporation land, 60 rather than 16 feet from the Rectory. Faced with this rebuff, Irvine took to the public arena and wrote a letter to the *Essex Standard*. Its last paragraph was to prove historic:

"I do not ask the public to interfere for the sake of myself or for any private person. But, if they think that it is as foolish to plant your Water Tower in the middle of your town as to put your Railway Station half a mile from it; if they do not desire for all time to block the extension of our noble High Street to the west; if they would be spared the painful reverberations of St Peter's bells against this "Jumbo"; and if they wish to reduce to a minimum in the future both risk and compensation for damage; I hope they will, without delay, put pressure upon the Corporation, and get them to consider the matter once more deliberately before taking a final and irretrievable step".[14]

Unfortunately, as we have seen, the irrevocable step was taken, but, perhaps to his own surprise, Irvine had coined a name.

Everyone knew 'Jumbo', London Zoo's most famous elephant, the largest it had ever owned, which had just been sold amid national protests to the American circus proprietor, P.T. Barnum. Somehow 'Jumbo' exactly described the monstrous construction on four legs, soon to loom over the town, glaringly functional, so obviously at odds with the fine line of the High Street and the 'period' charm so carefully cultivated at the west end of town. Irvine's letter and his subsequent appearance to protest before the full Council finally gave momentum to the rising misgivings of the town. Laughter is a powerful political weapon. 'Jumbo' poems appeared in the press, 'Jumbo' jokes at the theatre, and even the *Essex Standard* which had so far stuck by its claim of 1879 that the purchase of the Waterworks was not a party matter, had by 1883 come out in open criticism.[15]

Amidst this rising tide of hostility, the Waterworks Committee, still absorbing the implication of Clegg's admissions, reached the equally disturbing conclusion that they must seek another loan: the sixth to date. The interest on this, Fred Philbrick warned, would probably mean that the Waterworks' accounts would run at a loss for several years. Conscious of the effect this news might have upon the town (and on the November elections) he therefore proposed that the Waterworks deficit should be lost in the general borough account, that Parliamentary powers should be sought to consolidate the entire borough debt. This interesting expedient, which might today be justified on the ground that the water supply, like the new sewerage system, was a public service which the public should not expect to be run solely on the profit motive, was rejected by a large and representative *ad hoc* Committee that met on several occasions. It certainly appears that legal rather than financial or ideological arguments governed this decision. The Waterworks Committee therefore had no alternative but to go once more, cap in hand, to the Local Government Board for a further £5,000. Vainly they asked if this could be arranged without another Public Enquiry. Sternly the Local Government Board said no. There were just two weeks to the official opening.[16]

They all came to the Public Enquiry. Wicks was there and Clegg; John Bawtree Harvey and Fred Philbrick; Wilson Marriage, Henry Jones and all the Conservative 'hawks'. The Rural Dean of course was there, and opened up in language so warm that he was publicly rebuked by the Government Inspector. "I wish", said Fred Philbrick, who was deaf, "I could hear you so well at church". But increasingly the Public Enquiry became a public trial of the Waterworks Committee. Henry Jones, who lived at Lexden, asked whether it was not true (he knew it was) that the Corporation was now obliged to provide water to both Lexden and Mile End. Would not this involve further expense? Even another water-tower? Soon the Inspector himself was asking awkward questions. Gradually it emerged that the combination of the new borehole and the enlarged rising main was putting the two pumping engines, installed by Bruff less than ten years before, under such strain that they could barely cope. If just one broke down, observed a Conservative wag, Jumbo might prove rather a white elephant. For herein lay the Catch 22 at which the Council had arrived: the expenditure on Clegg's tower had been so great that even the £5,000 about to be borrowed was already spoken for. Yet without new engines and increased pumping power, Jumbo, the second largest water-tower in England was too small, its 230,000 gallon tank unable to meet the peak demands of all the town.[17]

As a matter of fact, the situation was even worse than had been admitted. The summer of 1883 was very dry and the demand of all the new customers was very great. Only three weeks before the Public Enquiry the new borehole had sucked dry and clogged up with sand. In desperate straits and without permission Clegg reconnected the supply from Sheepen Spring which, you recall, the Council had given up upon the completion of the new bore. By a nice irony the Sheepen Spring was owned by Alderman Papillon, Lord of the Manor of Lexden, to whom a telegram was sent requesting permission to re-use his spring. Permission was granted, but only for two weeks. Unhappily for the Waterworks Committee Alderman Papillon had just concluded a new contract to supply this pure spring water to the Great Eastern Railway for washing down their locomotives and filling up their boilers. It was fortunate indeed that the weather broke and heavy and unseasonal rain in early September raised the water table in the chalk once more. This however did not remove the fear that these events might one day repeat themselves, even though the well head was quickly lowered and the pumps sunk a further ten feet into the ground.[18]

Against this ominous background the official opening of the tower was held on September 27th 1883. Already it was over a year since building had commenced. The commemorative plaque, carved optimistically in 1882 and still standing above the entrance, thus records Jumbo's conception not his birth, the gestation period of an elephant being, after all, some 20 months. By an appropriate turn of fortune the opening ceremony was performed by the mayor, none other than John Bawtree Harvey, now elevated as a Liberal alderman. His presence did much to dignify the occasion and give it a sense of history, particularly as he recalled the pioneer efforts of Henry Webbe and John Wheeley 350 years before. He was however careful to avoid any reference to that more recent historical goal, a constant supply.

Jumbo's official opening, September 27th 1883. Bawtree Harvey wears the Mayor's chain; on his left Henry Goody; to his right in a white topper, Sir Robert Rawlinson; between them the diminutive head of Charles Clegg; far left, the other white topper is worn by James Wicks. One fifth of the Borough police force guards the entrance, doubtless to prevent the theft of a misleading commemorative plaque.

Instead he sought to invest this uneasy civic occasion with some civic pride. The tower, he reminded them, was all the work of local craftsmen: the design by Clegg, the brickwork by Everetts, the tank by Mumfords. This over-simplification kept from posterity the fact that the plates of the tank were cast in Newcastle, arriving at the Hythe with a consignment of coke. Mumford's contribution was to bolt them in place. Indeed Harvey omitted a good deal from his elegant speech, as most of his audience to a varying degree were aware. He was however able to indulge the Victorian love of statistics. The tower, he noted, was constructed from 1,200,000 bricks, 400 tons of cement and 369 tons of stone. The whole weighed 5,000 tons, of which 1,000 tons were water, so that the tank when full had to withstand 3,000 tons of pressure. Fortunately, perhaps, the Rural Dean was not listening. Indeed what no one could fail to notice, and the *Essex Standard* made the burden of its opening paragraph, was the absence from the ceremony of almost all the town's Conservatives or, as they put it, "the leading gentry and tradesmen of the town". Even the Corporation flag above Jumbo, it was noted, was flying at half mast.

Also addressing the assembly on that September morning were the Chairman of the Waterworks Committee, Councillor Wicks, and the guest of honour, Sir Robert Rawlinson, chief engineer to the Local Government Board which had, in several instalments, financed the tower. Wicks's speech was predictably political. Returning to his theme that the Waterworks would prove a profitable investment, he quoted extensively from speeches by Henry Jones to demonstrate the bi-partisan approach that had marked the original purchase. Sir Robert Rawlinson, himself a survivor from the great public health debate of 1847-48, and a loyal supporter of the now discarded Edwin Chadwick, lectured the town on the price that must be paid for pure water and made his memorable claim for Jumbo's probable longevity. He also urged the town to consider next the purchase of the Gas Company, until James Wicks pointed out that the Chairman was standing next to him.[19]

Indeed, the quiet and untroubled progress of the Gas Company throughout the 1880s is both a tribute to the skilled management of Harvey and his fellow directors, and a stark contrast to the public agonies of the municipal water supply. True, there were complaints about gas prices, but by installing new plant and benefitting from an increased income from their by-products, the Company were soon able to reduce the price to the consumer while still paying handsome dividends to their shareholders. Doubtless with a particular sense of satisfaction, they even paid an additional dividend to cover the barren year of 1879 which had precipitated the submission of their infamous revised Act. Even the rival threat of electricity was brushed aside and the Colchester Gas Company was to remain a private concern until nationalisation in 1948.[20] However one is bound to wonder whether the progress of the 1880s would have been so sweet and uneventful if, freed from the restraint of expectant shareholders, the Gas Company had become a political football or the object of an enthusiastic drive to improve it as a public service. Did municipalisation, involving as it did the hot hand of politics, always facilitate an improved service? It would be interesting to test this suggestion against the experience of other towns. Certainly the experience of Colchester demonstrates the problems that municipalisation was apt to bring, when hostility to rising rates was as old as local government and expectations of falling prices as an index of progress was a characteristic of the Victorian Age. Perhaps it also illustrates, as its protagonists always argued, that water was a special case. Even if street lamps were an essential aid to safety and a marginal deterrent against crime, the vital issues of public health and fire prevention were more truly a question of life and death. This and the question of profitability could explain why between 1845 and 1885 far more English towns took over their waterworks than took over their gas companies.[21]

And yet events in Colchester might easily have been otherwise. Had the Waterworks been run by a board of Colchester merchants, had William Hawkins lived, had Bruff not been so beset by rival commitments, had Harvey and his friends not rescued the Gas Company in 1865 and had the opposition to the Gas Company Bill succeeded in 1875, either or both utilities might have experienced a different fate. There are doubtless towns in England whose gas company was municipalised but whose waterworks were not. This underlines how little municipalisation was a question of ideology. In Colchester, at least, local circumstances, even personalities, provide a better explanation. But if municipalisation was not grounded in ideology, ideology as we shall now see, was certainly going to be affected by municipalisation.

R stands for RATES, which were something to
   sigh at,
So bloated they grew on a Liberal diet ;
But a healthy REDUCTION was soon brought
   about,
When the RATEPAYERS bundled the RADICALS
   out.

9

1885-1895: Civic Responsibilities

Controversy did not end with Jumbo's opening. Before long the *Essex Standard* was claiming that such was the fear that the overworked engines might collapse, that Jumbo was not being used at all and its tank was half empty. A long and acrimonious correspondence followed in the press between James Wicks and Henry Jones, who despite ignoring certain facts and claiming much from hindsight, emerged decidedly the better from the argument. His revelations make it clear that, up until his resignation, the Myland scheme had still been seriously considered, though his disinterestedness is somewhat challenged by his claim that Edward Easton had initially sought to put a water-tower on the site of the recently demolished Butt Road windmill, a property owned by Henry Jones himself.[1]

Then, seven weeks after its opening, Jumbo's essential services were put to a vital test. A serious fire broke out in Long Wyre Street where once the Romans had installed a piped supply. It was 54 minutes before any water was available. The equivalent delay in 1879 which, you recall, had led directly to the Waterworks purchase, had been 45 minutes. This did not do much for municipalisation or for the Colchester Liberal Party, particularly when it emerged that the cause was that old evil, the zoning of the town, which Jumbo's failure to provide a constant supply had consequently perpetuated. Nor did it help when it also emerged that the supply to Long Wyre Street should have been manually turned on by two Waterworks employees, Hayward and Balls, who had been found, later that night, barely coherent, in the appropriately named 'Spread Eagle' pub, run as a side-line by Hayward, the senior turncock. Hayward was sacked, but promptly carried off his turncock key, handing it over to his new employer, the Essex and Suffolk Fire Office. Clearly that responsible body had equal misgivings about municipal policy in the event of fire.[2]

Notwithstanding these embarrassments, the Borough Surveyor, Charles Clegg, requested, in recognition of his service to the Borough, a rise in salary. In the political circumstances this was hardly feasible, but it could not be disputed that his do-it-ourselves water and sewerage schemes had saved the Borough a considerable outlay in professional fees. Wicks bravely insisted that this should be recognised and a payment to Clegg of 200 guineas was made. Clegg duly pocketed this emolument and, within a year, left for a job overseas.[3]

All this and more spelt nemesis for poor old Wicks. In vain did he protest that the purchase of the Waterworks had been as much a Conservative as a Liberal decision. In the 1884 Borough elections the People's Candidate was defeated for the seat he had held for 12 years by Thomas Moy the Conservative and by a junior Liberal candidate, standing for office for the first time. That junior however was James Paxman, Colchester's most able businessman and by now an engineer of national reputation. The yawning gap and strange silence left by Wicks's defeat was filled in one respect: Paxman took over as Chairman of the Waterworks Committee. His superior skills at public relations helped to remove the pressure on the Liberal Party, but at any time during the next ten years, the very word 'Jumbo' was enough to leave Conservative audiences rolling in the aisles, and Liberals crawling off for cover.[4] Nor was Paxman, the town's leading engineer, to be free from the problems that had continuously beset the Waterworks affairs; nor did political behaviour improve.

Although the Conservatives had regained their traditional majority, they were unable in 1885 to prevent the return of James Wicks to the Council chamber. Instead, using their block vote, they barred him from all the key committees. Thus circumscribed, Wicks reacted somewhat like a wounded bull. Council meetings became slanging matches and partisan brawling reached its nadir at the ceremonial appointment of Henry Laver as mayor. An able local doctor, a distinguished natural historian and archaeologist, Laver is still regarded as one of the fathers of the Colchester and Essex Museum. He had however been a leading opponent of James Wicks, who consequently used this traditionally dignified occasion to launch a vituperative attack upon Laver's suitability for the office. Voices rose and so did councillors, and amidst the mêlée cries of "protect the mayor" were duly reported in the press.[5]

Out of such disgraceful scenes emerged what was called "the municipal compromise", an agreement, duly voted upon, to avoid personalities, keep politics out of decision-making and allocate council seats between the parties without resorting to elections, a process which inevitably heightened political controversy. This conspiracy of the élite was partly a cynical acknowledgement of a political stalemate. It was also the work of those more dignified councillors who were shocked by ungentlemanly conduct which, fully reported in the press, lowered their corporate dignity in an increasingly respectable and status-conscious age. This view was particularly held by a new brand of councillors who saw in their election to the Corporation as much a recognition of their economic leadership of the town as of their party affiliations, fixed though these were. James Paxman was one; so was Edwin Sanders, wholesale grocer, who, moving in on some of the tangled finances inherited from the Liberal regime, was soon being dubbed Colchester's Chancellor of the Exchequer. Paxman also made it clear that if the Borough wished to retain the services of so busy a man as he, they must not expect him to devote his time to contested elections every three years, the sort of accommodation which had hitherto been reserved for the likes of Alderman Papillon.

Businessmen conducting the business of Colchester – a fit and proper Victorian solution, for frequently during these years councillors can be heard proclaiming that they should set the same standards in the conduct of municipal affairs "as they would in their own businesses". Viewed in this light, that misleading term 'municipal socialism', should be renamed municipal capitalism and seen less as the precursor of 20th-century collectivism, and more as the logical extension of 19th-century economics. To the Conservatives of Colchester the Liberals' crime had been, not that they were champions of change or even of improvement, but that they were bad businessmen. And furthermore, as the new 'Chancellor' Edwin Sanders, was given to pointing out, they had left the books in a terrible state. Secretly, James Paxman had agreed with him; and there is a clear hint of surprise in his voice, as well as a spirited defence of his committee, when, soon after taking over the affairs of the Waterworks, he asserted:

EDWIN SANDERS (1848-1901), wholesale grocer and 'Chancellor of the Exchequer' contemplates the beauty of double entry bookeeping. Such symmetry doubtless inspired the rule imposed on his domestics to climb the stairs on the left and descend on the right, thereby prolonging the life of the carpet.

"He must say . . . the way in which the books were kept, and matters looked into was, in his opinion, creditable. Everything was done in a most businesslike way".[6]

Such local events could carry national significance. For the

Conservatives of Colchester were quietly staking out new ground that depended not a little on the theft of Liberal clothing. No longer able to maintain their once exclusive control over the Corporation through patronage and social superiority, they now proclaimed their ability to effect improvements in the running of the community in a more businesslike way than their opponents. Thus was the ground prepared for the 20th-century Conservative Party to be the natural home of businessmen. Nothing symbolised this transformation more succinctly, or dealt the Liberals a more telling blow, then the sight of Joseph Chamberlain, the 'millionaire' screw manufacturer, the hammer of the aristocracy and the prophet of municipal socialism, co- regent with Lord Salisbury of the obligingly renamed Unionist Party, a defection from the ranks of Liberalism that won the support of both Bawtree Harvey and James Paxman.[7]

The "municipal compromise" at Colchester was thus in large part a product of what we might call the Jumbo factor. Having subtly changed the rules, the Conservatives now faced the problem that Corporation debts and engineering complexities did not depart before political majorities. Just how big these two problems had now become needs to be carefully spelt out.

First, let us examine engineering complexities. During the late 1880s, Colchester was lucky to get by without a major breakdown in the water supply. Confident in the capacity of their new artesian bore, the Waterworks Committee had given up all significant auxiliary supplies. Thus throughout these years they had no alternative whatsoever should the borehole once more fill with mud. Their only standby was one half of the old Chiswell Meadow supply, still producing its 19,000 gallons a day. In terms of Colchester's needs this was negligible and those needs were constantly growing. Besides the obligation to extend the public supply to Lexden and Mile End, there was the growing number of applications from new customers as standards rose and speculative building continued in the town. It is dangerous to look too readily for conspiracies, but one is struck during the last days of the Liberals, by the large number of active Conservative landlords whose strident requests for water fill the pages of the minute book of the Waterworks Committee. One man certainly conducted a sustained campaign. Henry Jones regularly refused to pay water rates when they were raised, bickered over the water supply to Lexden and demanded the installation of water mains along Salisbury Avenue long before he had built any of its houses.[8]

To meet these growing needs, at great cost in fuel and repair bills, Bruff's old engines were worked almost night and day. Between 1879 and 1884, under Wicks and the Liberals, the weekly output of water had risen by 32%, while the number of domestic customers had increased by 33%. Little prospect here of extending a period of supply which ranged between 8 and 10 hours a day, depending where you lived. During the next five years (1884-89) when the Conservatives were in command and Paxman was Chairman of the Waterworks Committee, the number of customers rose a further 23%, but the volume of water did not. An actual decrease in the daily quantity to domestic consumers was only prevented by terminating a contract with the Great Eastern Railway, which accounted for almost 10% of total output. Worst of all, by the summer of 1889, the new artesian bore was clearly faltering. The water table fell, and the total annual output for 1889 was actually less than it had been in 1884.[9]

Faced with this crisis, Paxman called in an expert, a young engineer called Mackworth Wood, recommended to Paxman through his professional connections. Wood's Reports of 1889, 1890 and 1891 make clear the continuing problems of the Waterworks. Firstly, the town was still riddled with narrow-bore mains, and since the network had been extended over many years and in a distinctly haphazard way, there was no proper circuit system and many dead ends. Even if there had been a constant supply, much of the town would not have received an adequate flow of water. Secondly, as everyone knew, the existing engines were now inadequate. Day after day Jumbo steadily emptied as demand from the town exceeded the pumping speed of the engines and the current yield of the well. Only cutting off the supply to parts of the town during the afternoon prevented the tank from running dry. Wood was therefore amazed to discover that Jumbo had never been allowed to get more than three quarters full. For despite the fact that the original wrought iron design had been replaced by cast iron plates 1.5 inches thick; despite the fact that these plates had been reinforced by Paxman with 25 metal stays; and despite the fact that Jumbo had survived the 1884 Colchester earthquake with only hairline cracks, the Waterworks Committee had secretly dreaded that Canon Irvine's worst fears and loudest predictions might one day actually come true.[10]

As an immediate solution Wood proposed the sealing off of Bruff's original bore and the sinking of the new well-head and pumps a further 89 feet. Paxman overruled this proposal, presumably on the grounds of safety, and a compromise depth of 79 feet was settled on. Considering that the well was the town's only supply and would thus have to be fully functioning throughout, one can only be impressed that this hazardous operation was successfully carried out. Such measures were of course merely a holding operation. A sense of obligation to balance the books and a fear of the political consequences kept Paxman and his Committee from the greater but necessary step of installing new engines. Paxman himself always insisted that Bruff's engines could be made to last for several more years, but a detailed look at the financial restraints they now faced provides a better explanation.[11]

Buying the Waterworks and building Jumbo had cost over

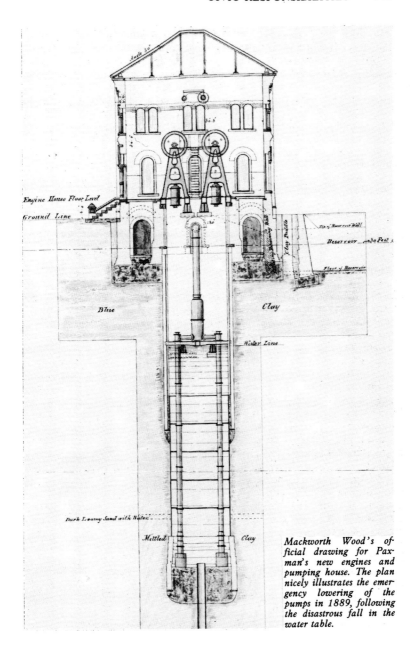

Mackworth Wood's official drawing for Paxman's new engines and pumping house. The plan nicely illustrates the emergency lowering of the pumps in 1889, following the disastrous fall in the water table.

£100,000. Thus during the 1880s the Waterworks Committee had to find nearly £6,000 in interest and repayment from a gross revenue of £6,500. No wonder the water rate went up. Wicks's "profitable investment", on which Peter Bruff had allegedly made a clear profit of £2,900 during his last year of ownership, was, when James Paxman took over the Committee, running an annual deficit of £500. It did not help that at the same time the town was also committed to the large expense of new main drainage and sewage works. By 1885 the town's public health debt was £148,000, sone £127,000 of which, borrowed at the high interest rate of 4.5%, came from the Public Works Loan Commissioners on behalf of the Local Government Board. This sum was exceeded by only seven other local authorities in Britain. Considering that the Borough Council's indebtedness prior to the purchase of the Waterworks had been a single loan of £5,000, one begins to see what a revolution this represented in local government and with what dramatic suddenness Colchester entered the field of municipal trading.[12] Yet during the mid 1880s the town was also establishing a public recreation ground and bathing place, considering a public library, preparing for a steam tramway, attempting to be the first town in England to establish a house-to-house electricity supply and planning to build a new Town Hall, since the existing one, besides being too small, was clearly falling apart. True, most of these schemes were postponed or abandoned, but together they represent an explosion in Council activity, as responsibilities continued to accrue. By 1908 the Council had added electricity, tramways, education and a library to its duties, and the Corporation debt topped £460,000.[13]

The completion of the new sewage works provides interesting parallels with the water question. Here too there were expenses beyond what was expected, here too technical complications arose to mock the politicians' optimism. Forced into action by the millers' prosecution, the Town Council, upon Clegg's advice, adopted a system based on vast settling beds. The opening of the new works, attended like Jumbo's opening by Sir Robert Rawlinson, had some very embarrassing moments. As the great man peered at the clotted liquid emerging from the new pumping station, there was little doubt in the minds of the gathered dignitaries what it reminded them of. They had only to sniff for confirmation. The whole expensive sewage system was, in short, a decided failure. The human effluent of Colchester hitherto channeled by sewers into various parts of the river, now lay in fetid pools at the Hythe, before disgorging from a vast pipe to drift up or down the lower river according to the state of the tide. When the wind was in the wrong direction, or on a still summer's day, the smell among the largely working class community of Hythe Hill was all-pervasive.[14]

To rescue the working classes there arose another embattled rector. Beneath the headline, "The Bitter Cry of Outcast Colchester", the Rev.

Dr Manning of St Leonards-at-the-Hythe reflected in his indignation for the medical vulnerability of the poor the Rural Dean's concern for the aesthetic sensitivity of the rich. Despite the sharp criticism of his near neighbour, James Paxman, Manning stuck by the popular belief that nasty smells could of themselves generate disease. Spies were mounted on the sewer outfall pipes and war was declared upon the Borough's Main Drainage Committee. Partly on principle, partly in exasperation, the Liberal chairman persuaded most of the Committee, Liberals and Conservatives alike, to join him in resignation, a step unprecedented in the Borough's history. Lamenting that political controversy was making the already difficult job of civic responsibility

The municipal line-up for the opening of the Sewage Works, July 31st, 1884. Beneath the new pumping station stand, from the left, 1st James Paxman, 3rd Edward Marriage with white beard and quaker hat, 5th Fred Philbrick, 6th Sir Robert Rawlinson, 7th James Wicks, 8th Wilson Marriage, 9th Dr. Brown, the Medical Officer of Health, 10th Thomas Moy, 12th the mayor, Alfred Francis, with Edwin Sanders just above him. Second from the right is thought to be Arthur Mumford, with Charles Clegg the figure behind at the doorway.

intolerable, he did not even recontest his council seat. Thus was a seat left vacant for James Wicks to return to office. This irony was compounded by another: the resigning Chairman was Councillor Wilson Marriage, whose prosecution of the Corporation had, so to speak, first activated the sewerage question. Eventually under the new 'Chancellor', Edwin Sanders, the settling beds were removed and a chemical process, not unlike that proposed by Mr Hillé ten years before, was installed.[15]

DR. FREDERICK MANNING, quick with a contemporary allusion, rendered public 'The Bitter Cry of Outcast Colchester' against the by-products of activated sludge, and "the foul effluvia issuing from the sewer opening at my own gate".

It is against this background that councillors of both parties began to see themselves not just as rival protagonists for political gain, but as the dignified managers of the town's affairs. For five years not a single Council seat was contested, as leading Liberals who had lost their seats in the political punch-ups of 1882-84 were eased back on to the Council, unchallenged by the Conservatives. The Conservatives even resisted an attempt from below by small shopkeepers in their own party to disrupt this consensus (and the tone of the membership) by putting forward their own candidate in a seat earmarked for a banker newly settled in the town. Of course the political truce did not last for ever. In 1890 parties and personalities once more burst into life, but now the accumulating burden of committee work forced a Council equally divided between Liberals and Conservatives to get on with the job. The scale of this transformation, symbolised by a growing tendency to refer to the Town Council as "our local Parliament", needs to be quantified.[16]

For most of the period covered by this book the Corporation had boasted two active committees and so late as 1871 the full Council met only quarterly. Ten years later it frequently met twice a month, while the number of committees rose to 12 in 1880 and 16 in 1890. Even unenthusiastic councillors might be called out on several evenings a week. No wonder that when in 1892 the Council took over the remaining duties of the Commissioners, its size was for the first time increased from 24 to 32 members. A new professionalism governed its affairs as printed minutes, agendas and reports began to proliferate and a corresponding expansion of Town Hall staff took place. Fortunately, perhaps, the burden of organisation no longer rested on the ageing shoulders of Fred Philbrick. He was replaced by Henry C. Wanklyn, the town's first modern Town Clerk. Wanklyn was probably a Conservative by persuasion, but if so, it did not obtrude on his discreet and efficient conduct of his job. He had no private practice and, unlike his two predecessors, never voiced opinions except when asked and did not enter into debate at Council meetings.

Remarkable reconciliations followed. With much back-slapping and expressions of regret, Charles Henry Hawkins, fully recovered in health, was reinstated as an alderman. Even James Wicks was forgiven. With tears in his eyes, he became an alderman too by the unanimous decision of both Liberals and Conservatives, a promotion which he regarded as a greater honour than that of mayor, an office now reckoned to cost the incumbent £1,500 a year in hospitality.[17]

For civic pomp was on the increase, most evidently in the annual Oyster Feast which, graced by ever more distinguished special guests,

JAMES PAXMAN, Colchester's most popular (and most generous) late Victorian mayor, experienced far more problems as Chairman of the Waterworks Committee.

became a great gathering of the town's élite, where loyalty to the Queen, the greatness of Britain and the "dear old Borough" replaced any hint of political contention. In 1887 Colchester, swept like the rest of Britain on a tide of patriotic enthusiasm, celebrated Queen Victoria's Jubilee. In November of that year, James Paxman, though a Liberal, was elected mayor by a Conservative majority, the first time this had happened in the history of the Corporation. Thereafter the mayoralty alternated between the parties, regardless of majorities. Faced with the management of the town's affairs, Liberals and Conservatives had little to divide them. Yet both, as employers, viewed with misgiving or alarm the rise in Colchester of organised labour and militant Trade Unionism in the 1890s. Certainly James Paxman, the town's leading employer, even James Wicks, the People's Alderman, would rather do without class war in industry, preferring the paternalism which the Town Council, self-perpetuating but concerned, essentially epitomised.[18] Viewed in this light the debate about the 'inevitability' of the Labour Party should perhaps be linked with municipal trading, and the easy amalgamation of the Liberal and Conservative leadership in many provincial towns during and after the First World War, now that their outstanding religious and educational disagreements had become irrelevant, can be more readily understood.

Indeed the relationship of municipal action to the joint but separate issues of enlightening and controlling the working classes deserves a little attention. So early as 1858, Harvey had argued in his pamphlet to the Commissioners that

> ". . . it must not be forgotten that where filth abounds, disorder and intemperance . . . are sure to discover themselves . . . The question is an important one, and affects not only the health, but also the character of the community".[19]

As a leading evangelical, Harvey was genuinely concerned for the moral enlightenment and physical well-being of the poor, but it did not escape the notice of ratepayers and employers that the absorption of middle-class values by the lower orders invariably produced not only sobriety and self-esteem but punctuality and respect for authority too. In short, there was more than one implication to the Victorian maxim that cleanliness was next to godliness.

And when we seek the origins, twenty-five years later, of a more energetic public policy in the town, we should remember that the well-being and reliability of their workers was the daily concern of most public men in their private capacity as employers. It was a policy which paid dividends, as the many mansions behind Lexden Road still eloquently testify. Equally significant are the rows of semi-detached villas in New Town, where so many of their senior employees lived. For the marked increase in the housing stock after 1875, coupled with the growing number of commercial and industrial premises, inevitably increased the borough's rateable value.[20] Thus was progress funded without too great a challenge to that old bugbear, hostility to rising rates. Equally helpful was the public behaviour of the town's élite. That the owners of large businesses should retain so large a share of the wealth that they generated, encouraged on their part those acts of public charity that for centuries had been instruments of both social control and social appeasement. There were few more generous supporters of the Essex and Colchester Hospital than James Wicks or Charles Henry Hawkins, and no one did more to popularise the collections on 'Hospital Saturday' than their fellow Governor, James

Paxman. The Public Recreation Ground and the new Bathing Place owed much to generous donations by members of the business community, while the new Public Library, twice blocked by ratepayer resistance, was finally justified by a £1,000 bequest from a one-time resident of the town. For 22 years Colchester was spared the 'expense' of an elected School Board, when, faced by nonconformist reluctance, some resolute Anglican fund-raising provided sufficient additional schooling in the Borough, one of the last examples of genuine sectarian division in the town.[21]

Organised sport, improving literature and elementary education were not only worthy outlets for charity but admirable agencies for inculcating in the lower classes those necessary virtues of discipline, fair play and respect for higher wisdom. So was that essential element of a structured society: civic pomp and ceremony. An annual opportunity was provided by the Colchester Oyster Feast, a celebration reckoned to cost the mayor in person over £1,000. Yet leading members of the business community, who might as private citizens vigorously resist any increase in the rateable value levied on their factories, willingly footed the Oyster Feast bill when their turn came to be mayor.[22] Nor was this all: extensions to the hospital, the opening of a Soldiers' Home, the conversion of the old Corn Exchange into the Albert School of Science and Art, the presentation of the Castle Park to the town, each an example of directed public charity, were all made the occasion of public ceremonies, invariably graced by leading national figures or even members of the royal family. The presence of a resident garrison provided the added spectacle of generals on horseback and redcoat soldiers lining the route, presenting arms as the cavalcade of carriages arrived from the railway station. The well-behaved spectators could only wonder and admire.[23]

Similar efforts were made to give a local emphasis to the celebration of the Royal Jubilees of 1887 and 1897. Newspapers reported in detail the lavish decorations on leading shops and businesses, adding the admiring comments of visitors from London, amazed by all they saw. Committees of leading citizens planned for weeks in advance a programme of processions and entertainments, the unwritten theme of which might be 'the town as a community'. The result of so much corporate energy was wholly satisfactory. Addressing a banquet laid on for Mr Paxman's employees, the mayor was able to boast:

"I think it is in a great measure owing to the very good terms on which most - I may say all - of the large employers of labour in this town are with their men, that we have such a happy community as we certainly have in this town. I say it without fear of contradiction, that this is one of the most orderly towns for its size in England".

Colchester, Water Tower, "Jumbo"

SANITARY ARCHITECTURE. Left, Jumbo stands reflected in the murky waters of Dodd's clay reservoir, standing inside the Balkerne Gate. This continued to supply water to British Rail until 1956. Above, the pumping station of the Sewage Works, 1884 and below the Waterworks pumping station, opened by Paxman in 1894.

It only needed Councillor Wilson Marriage, in proposing a toast to the Mayor and Corporation, to point up the benefits of pure water, good drainage and low rates that underpinned this corporate bliss.

Nothing symbolised more vividly the enhanced status of the Corporation than the lavish grandeur of the new Town Hall, built in the first years of the 20th century. Opened by Lord Rosebery, the Liberal Prime Minister, it was, appropriately, the current mayor, Wilson Marriage, otherwise rejoicing in the bizarre title and quaint garments of the Port Reeve, who supervised the ceremony. Colchester's grandest building cost £55,000, £12,000 of which was subscribed by local benefactors, a final act of public charity to this embodiment of civic pride.[24]

The last chapter in the water question was written by James Paxman, who, like Peter Bruff and Mrs Hawkins, had sufficient confidence in the Waterworks to invest in it himself, personally meeting one of the several £2,500 loans that the project still required. By carefully husbanding income and building up a loyal Committee of several leading businessmen, Paxman was able to finance the lowering of the pumps and the replacement of a large quantity of the unsatisfactory mains. In 1892 he secured approval from the Council for a £12,000 loan from the Local Government Board to finance new high-speed engines, new premises and a new rising main to Jumbo. The premises were completed in 1894 and in modified form still stand at the foot of Balkerne Hill today. To celebrate these landmarks Paxman was wont to treat his entire committee to afternoon tea in the small viewing room on top of Jumbo, which had once been nicknamed "Wick's folly". On a beautiful clear day sailing ships and yachts were clearly visible off the coast from Brightlingsea. Who knows but Peter Bruff, still active in old age, was helming one?[25]

If, however, Paxman carefully cultivated his Committee, he was less successful with the remainder of the Council. Early in 1895 the revelation that the new engines and new works had cost considerably more than had been estimated and would require fresh borrowing, led to renewed outbreaks of protest in the Council chamber. After 15 years of public ownership, it was claimed, the Waterworks still had debts of over £100,000, and had yet to save a penny off the rates, while Paxman and his Committee were a closed body and a law unto themselves, for ever coming to the Council for more subsidies and loans. A mighty row followed, and the old evil of personalities raised its ugly head. It might have been 1884 all over again, except in one respect. This time the Council was not split on party lines; it was the Waterworks Committee, most of them, whether Liberal or Conservative, personal friends of Paxman, under attack from other, mostly more recent, members of the Council. Of course the loans were, in the end, sanctioned (a further £6,250), but niggling continued over fences and sheds in the best spirit of the parish pump. There was little doubt however that this last expenditure had introduced major cost-saving benefits. The new engines were tested, and registered a full 50% improvement on their predecessors. This was in part due to the installation of the world famous 'Economic' boilers, manufactured by Paxman's own firm, a transaction he was careful to render legal and free from all but a minimum profit.[26]

And so at long, long last a constant supply of water could be provided to the town. And it is only appropriate that this was achieved in December 1895, one month after James Wicks finally became the mayor of Colchester, and sixteen years after the ex-Chairman of the Waterworks Committee had first set out to provide it. Only the installation of waste detectors the following year was required to eliminate an annual loss of 73,000,000 gallons caused by leaking pipes. The story begun in 1847, if not in Roman times, had ended. Before the old queen died, the assiduous Medical Officer of Health for Essex, Dr Thresh, was able to report that Colchester now had 37.5 miles of water mains compared to the 16 miles it had possessed when the Waterworks were purchased by the town, and that a constant supply now served 89% of the civilian population. In short

> "There is a plentiful supply of water and sufficient for many years to come . . . the Works are second to none in the Eastern Counties, and the character of the work is first class".[27]

In part one feels bound to say to this: and so they should have been. For between 1880 and 1895 virtually the entire system as left by Bruff and costing the Borough £87,000 had been replaced on a much more extensive scale for under £40,000, a figure which even includes the price of Jumbo. Not till 1930 was the purchase of the Waterworks finally paid for, let alone the innumerable subsequent loans. If the water question was, at the last, an engineering triumph, it was, to the end, a financial nightmare.[28]

D stands for DRAINS, so Defectively laid,
   And the two-hundred guinea DONATION we made.
Though it seems they were not very durable drains,
Still the drain on the purse of the public remains.

10

Old Mortality

After so long and expensive a journey, we should perhaps enquire how far the events of this narrative left their mark upon the public health of Colchester. A traditional approach is a comparison of death rates: the annual number of deaths per thousand of the population. These can be calculated from 1838 onwards when the registration of all births, marriages and deaths became compulsory. As a measuring device death rates are rather a blunt instrument, affected by such diverse factors as variations in the birth rate which govern the percentage of infants, the most vulnerable group in the population; the state and availability of housing stock; the incidence of local epidemics; and, above all, the general standard of living and diet in the community, which significantly affects its resistance to disease. All this will colour the statistics as well as environmental questions like the state of drainage, the adequacy of sewage disposal and the availability of pure water, issues with which this book has been concerned. It is also unwise in the 19th century to pay too much regard to the death rate of any given year. This was frequently a reflection of the weather. A long cold winter took its toll in deaths as did a long hot summer, when infectious diseases, brought on by bad hygiene, contaminated food and impure water, were doubly virulent. For this reason average figures over a five-year period should be used. There are also statistical considerations that should warn us against placing any emphasis on a single decimal place. Since a key factor in calculating death rates is the size of the population, and since this was only accurately recorded every ten years, an annual figure is inevitably an approximate calculation based on a likely figure for the middle of a given year. In Colchester there is an added hazard caused by the arrival of the Infantry Barracks in 1856 and the Cavalry Barracks in 1862. Appropriate adjustments are therefore necessary, even though, as a constantly mobile population, garrison figures ultimately defy accuracy.[1] The presence of the garrison also distorted the age and sex balance of the population, leading to further complications. Since women live longer than men, and children are more at risk than adults, a disproportionate number of adult males can falsify any calculations. Without sophisticated statistical adjustments these factors affect both birth and death rates. What we are studying are therefore named, very appropriately, crude death rates.

With these reservations in mind, Table 1 shows the quinquennial death rates for Colchester set beside the national figures and the figures for Leeds, a rapidly expanding industrial city whose sanitary condition John Simon, Chadwick's successor as guardian of the nation's health, once labelled "in proportion to the importance of the town . . . perhaps . . . the worst that has ever come to the knowledge of this department". More detailed annual figures for Colchester appear in Appendix A, page 150.

TABLE 1: Quinquennial Crude Death Rates [2]

Years	Colchester	England and Wales	Leeds
1838-40	27.7	22.4	33.0[a]
1841-45	23.1	21.4	27.5[b]
1846-50	24.0	23.3	30.0[c]
1851-55	22.7	22.7	31.5[d]
1856-60	21.1	21.8	27.7[e]
1861-65	21.1	22.6	29.7
1866-70	21.0	22.4	28.9
1871-75	19.7	22.0	27.9
1876-80	20.0	20.8	24.6
1881-85	17.8	19.4	22.9
1886-90	17.1	18.9	21.1
1891-95	17.3	18.7	21.1
1896-00	15.6	17.7	19.7

a = 1839-40	d = 1849-53
b = 1841-43	e = 1855-62
c = 1844-48	

Victorian Colchester was frequently described as a healthy town by its inhabitants. Set on a hill, with a well-drained soil, sloping down to a convenient river, its unhurried life-style, paved High Street and smart shops were frequently contrasted to the gloom of London or the squalor of a northern industrial city. In part, of course, this picture was a product of local pride, in part a publicity gesture to encourage the wealthy to settle in the town, thereby augmenting the rates, upholding property prices and adding to the tone of social life. Nevertheless this is a picture that is recognisable and, in the event, largely justified by the figures. As Britain became a predominantly urban nation so

Colchester's death rates sank below the national average and were always below those of an industrial city like Leeds or, to take a local example, the metropolitan borough of West Ham.[3] They also appear to have been low when we compare like with like. One of the more important publications of the public health campaign made a comparison of mortality rates in some 58 urban registration districts from all parts of England and Wales. They did not include Colchester, but they did feature some seven towns which by population and circumstance resembled Colchester. All seven were ancient towns, all were set on a river, most were committed by their history to a nucleated centre, and most, during the mid-Victorian years, served as a regional centre and market town, rather than a major industrial development. Table 2 shows their crude death rates for the decade 1851-60. Only one, Reading, has a rate below that of Colchester. Moreover of the remaining 51 districts listed in the original survey, only four, Cheltenham (19.0), Hastings (18.2), Caistor (18.8) and Lincoln (20.4), had lower rates than Colchester.

TABLE 2: Comparative Death Rates by Town[4]

Town	1851-61 Inter-Censual Population Increase	Estimated Mid-Censual Population	1851-61 Inter-Censual Deaths	1851-61 Crude Death Rate
Maidstone	+1,286	37,383	8,468	22.7
Worcester	+1,646	29,323	6,779	23.1
Shrewsbury	+1,340	24,444	6,156	25.2
Reading	+1,850	24,025	5,210	21.7
Stafford	+843	23,630	5,263	22.3
Canterbury	+1,271	15,371	3,517	22.9
Chichester	+168	14,606	3,193	21.9
Colchester	+2,100	21,590	4,707	21.8

If then we are talking about one of the less unhealthy towns in Victorian England, can we plot any correlation between the events of our narrative and the overall Colchester death rates? Or will these figures prove to be a mere reflection of the general level of diet and well-being among the bulk of the population - in short a crude indicator of the town's economic health?

The death rate for Colchester in 1838, the first year on record, was 30.7, an alarmingly high figure compared to a national rate of 22.4 for that year. Similarly the quinquennial average for 1838-42 was 25.5 compared to a national figure of 22.1, and a figure of 24.4 for Ipswich, Colchester's larger and faster growing neighbour.[5] How far this reflects poor environmental health, a poor diet, economic depression or the national typhus epidemic of 1837-38, or even a combination of all four, local sources do not make clear. Nor can we know accurate figures for the preceding years, but there is some ground for suspecting that they were no worse. In 1834 the town had endured its only serious cholera outbreak of the century. In two months there were 152 known cases and 91 ensuing deaths. In August, September and October there were 209 burials, the equivalent of a death rate of 50.2. To illustrate the severity of the outbreak the Commissioners included in a report the total burials recorded in the same three months for the years 1831, 1832 and 1833, but unfortunately we cannot be sure that nonconformist burials were included in these figures. Generally August to October were average months for mortality, and the figures quoted by the Commissioners would give death rates for all three years of under 23.0.[6]

If this were true, the high figures for 1838 to 1840 would cast interesting light on the main years of Chartist unrest. Insofar as crude death rates are a rough index of economic well-being, these years were exceptionally bad in Colchester, a typical market town with a less than buoyant economy. Thereafter things improved.

This thesis finds possible corroboration in another index of distress. During the winter months of 1838-41 strenuous and genuine efforts were made to raise donations to relieve the suffering of the poor by providing free coal, free blankets and free soup during those very months which produced the highest mortality figures. Indeed it is worth reflecting that the price of coal was probably a more significant factor in the health of the poor than the price of water. These relief measures could be on an extensive scale now that the new Poor Law placed such restrictions on 'outdoor relief'. During the long cold spell of January-February 1841 some £800 in all was raised in several instalments from donations by the well-to-do, door-to-door appeals and collections in churches. A portion was set aside to provide public works for destitute men, but the Committee was unable to cope with all the applications for work that they received. It was therefore decided to employ only unemployed married men with children to clear away the snow. In three days the numbers so employed were 140, 217 and 270, with an equal number of single men available, but not employed. Such evidence of widespread unemployment and distress led directly to the establishment of the Colchester Provident Labourers Society, an organisation which by collecting small sums from labourers throughout the year dispensed a greater value in coal and comfort to them during the winter months, the balance being met by public donations.[7]

When we turn to the death rates of the 1840s the picture is one of marginal improvement. The rate for the whole decade was 23.5, but this figure masks considerable annual variations, and a five-year period, 1844-48, which averaged 25.3. Indeed the figures would have been far worse had not Colchester been spared the great cholera outbreak of 1848-49. These were of course the years when, stimulated by a national campaign, loud complaints were first levelled at the old Waterworks Company and at the state of the public wells. The decade also saw the reconstitution of the Commissioners and their slow construction of a new system of main sewers, a programme completed in 1854. By this date Peter Bruff had also effected his transformation of the Waterworks with a new artesian bore and the initiation of a six-day a week supply. It is therefore very tempting to see some connection between these events and the fact that whereas, from 1838 to 1854, the annual death rate exceeded 23 per 1,000 on 12 of the 17 years, thereafter it did so only twice, in 1857 and 1863.[8]

Such statistical acrobatics should however be tempered by the thought, clearly brought out by Harvey's pamphlet and the work of the Commissioners, that only a fraction of the population lived in premises connected to the main sewers or served by the pipes of the Waterworks Company. It is easier to suggest that falling death rates also reflect an improving standard of living and a greater awareness of the virtues of cleanliness and nuisance removal. This would suggest that similar improvements were occuring nationally, but were masked in the statistics by the rapidly growing urban sector whose higher mortality rates the figures for Leeds strikingly illustrate.

Colchester's falling death rates during the period 1838 to 1854 render more telling the stationary death rates of the period 1855 to 1871. Significantly these were years when no great improvements were made either in the water supply or in the drainage and cleansing systems of the town. The number of new houses barely kept pace with the expansion of the population and Colchester remained predominantly a market town, slowly benefiting from the relative prosperity of agriculture during these years. Indeed the 1850s saw such an expansion of the traditional livestock market, held every Saturday in the High Street, that there was a growing demand supported by Bawtree Harvey and the sanitarians for its removal to a larger and more suitable site. A decade of wrangling followed before a 'new' market was opened at Middleborough, on a large open space at the bottom of North Hill.[9]

There is however one considerable complication to this period: the arrival of the Army. Rapidly rising to some 2,500 males and 500 females, the garrison soon represented over 12% of the population.

(Right). Part of a pamphlet printed by Bawtree Harvey in 1855, satirising the 'Dirty Party', who wished to retain the cattle market in the High Street. A good many of its supporters, however, came from his own Liberal Party. The designation CHURCH & FILTH is a double pun. Not only does it echo the Conservative motto "CHURCH & STATE", but a leading Colchester Conservative was Councillor John Church.

To the Electors of the
THIRD WARD.

GENTLEMEN,

As a Candidate for your votes at the forthcoming Municipal Election, I wish at once to state my views on the all-absorbing question of

THE CATTLE MARKET.

Believing that it is a blessing to the Town generally, and to the High Street in particular, and that the gases exhaled by the ordure deposited on the Saturday have a most salutary influence upon the atmosphere of Sunday and the succeeding days, I shall strenuously oppose any attempt to remove this time-honoured Institution, from whatever quarter it may come.

So strong are my feelings upon this vital question, that I should regret exceedingly the weekly removal of what I regard as good and wholesome aliment for the air, were it not that our loss as townspeople is compensated by the gain of

OUR COUNTRY FRIENDS.

For this, as for every other beneficent arrangement of our fore-fathers, you may rely upon my uncompromising advocacy.

I remain, Gentlemen,

Your obedient Servant,

CHURCH & FILTH.

Colchester, October 25th
1853.

Thereafter it constantly fluctuated as the following figures indicate:[10]

Date	Numbers[+]	% of Colchester Population
Feb. 1856	2,220	9.9
Sept. 1857	c.3,000	c.12.9
Census 1861	2,949	12.4
Census 1871	3,448	13.1
Census 1881	2,618	9.2
Census 1891	3,732	10.8
Census 1901	3,921*	10.2

[+] *These figures slightly underestimate the total as most of the officers and their families lived among the civilian population.*

* *Garrison numbers were untypically low at the 1901 census because of the current demands of the Boer War.*

The presence of over 2,000 unmarried men, mostly in the prime of life, grossly distorted the age and sex mix of the Colchester population. This could have had a significant effect upon the borough's death rate. According to one viewpoint, healthy and fit young men were less likely to die than the rest of the population. On the other hand there is evidence in the Colchester press that living conditions in the garrison were frequently less than ideal and epidemics, particularly during the middle Victorian years, often took a heavy toll.[11] Garrison numbers also affected that other key indicator, the birth rate. Table 3 gives the quinquennial crude birth rates for Colchester compared with the national figures:

TABLE 3: Quinquennial Crude Birth Rates [12]

	England and Wales	Colchester
1841-45	32.5	32.6
1846-50	32.8	33.7
1851-55	34.0	30.8
1856-60	34.4	30.4
1861-65	35.1	32.2
1866-70	35.3	31.3
1871-75	35.5	32.2
1876-80	35.4	32.3
1881-85	33.5	31.2
1886-90	31.4	28.9
1891-95	30.5	27.9
1896-00	29.3	26.3

From 1856 the Army was an important aspect of Colchester life. The prefabricated wooden huts of the Infantry Barracks, built originally for use by Belgian mercenaries in the Crimean War, provided 'temporary' accommodation until the 20th century.

A low birth rate usually had a benign effect upon the death rate, since infant mortality was always a major contributor to the total. Fewer infant births meant fewer infant deaths. During the 1850s Colchester's birth rate fell significantly below the national average. How far can this be attributed to an extensive garrison, few of whose residents had legitimate offspring?

Working from the 1871 census,[13] just over 800 of the Colchester garrison were women and children and some 300 were married men, leaving some 2,350 unmarried men. Rounding this upward to 2,500 (a generous figure) would produce a Colchester birth rate for 1861-70 of 35.3, compared with the actual rate of 31.7. This larger figure would match Colchester's birth rates of the 1840s which were slightly above the national average. It would also represent an additional 89 births a year, which, given the infant mortality rate for that decade of 146 per 1,000 would have increased the death rate from 21.1 to 21.5 per 1,000. This is not an overwhelming increase. Nor would it alter the general trend of a static death rate between 1855 and 1871. There is moreover a complication to the argument that the garrison reduced Colchester's overall death rate. The dramatic fall in the Colcheser birth rate occurs from 1852 onwards, four years before the arrival of the garrison. Why was this? There are reasons for believing that it was caused by the migration from the town of significant numbers of young men, usually in the direction of London.[14] Young women went too, but they were invariably replaced by others moving into the town from the surrounding villages to take up domestic service. Consequently there was at both the 1861 and 1871 censuses an excess of some 2,000 or 4.6% of women over men in the civilian population. Our final judgement must therefore be that the presence of the garrison was but one factor in Colchester's lower birth rates in this period, which were in turn a small but constant factor in the lower death rates that accompanied them.

As we move on into the 1870s we find a town that is at last beginning to enjoy modest economic growth. Doubtless as a consequence, the civilian population grew during this decade at a faster rate than for any previous ten-year period except the 1820s. The decade also witnessed Peter Bruff's more energetic approach to the services of the Waterworks Company, an extension to its operations that led nonetheless to municipal purchase in 1879. This too was the decade when the widespread adoption of the water closet and the consequent increase in river pollution reached a climax with the millers' prosecution of the town.

All this lends especial significance to the accompanying quinquennial death rates. Commentators have often noted that, for all the efforts of Chadwick and Simon, national death rates only began to fall in the second half of the 1870s.[15] Such was not the case in Colchester. Here crude death rates which had remained unchanged for 15 years improved significantly in the early 1870s only to deteriorate in the second quinquennium. This is so strikingly at variance with the national pattern and, for example, the city of Leeds, which also registered a sharp improvement after 1875, as to require a special explanation. And it is difficult not to point the finger at the river, or to suggest that during the 1870s Colchester was experiencing its own "great stink" 20 years after the City of London. For, during the long search for a suitable method of sewage disposal, forced on the town by the millers' prosecution, the point was several times made that Colchester was tackling the problem of sewage disposal "twenty years after other towns".[16] The delay may well have prevented costly failure; it may equally have increased the town's mortality.

This explanation is the more convincing when we consider the figures for the 1880s. The fall in death rates here is the most dramatic of the entire series, and this in a decade which witnessed the fastest population growth of the century. Colchester was now enjoying some economic prosperity and it is reasonable to conclude that overall diet improved as the town benefited from a national fall in food prices. More significantly this was the decade when the services of the Waterworks were extended to a far greater proportion of the population, and the new main sewerage system was completed. In justice to the harrassed Borough Council it should be noted that the quinquennium 1881-1885, which recorded the sharpest political controversy over public health, also recorded the sharpest fall in the death rate.

There is an additional consideration. This book has not discussed to any extent the quality of housing in the town at any given period, yet it is obvious that this was a significant contributor to the state of public health. All contemporary observers were agreed that the courts and alleyways of the poor were the worst haunts of dirt and of disease. These did not go away; but from the mid-1870s the quantity of new housing being built ensured that the expanding population of the town no longer expanded inwards. Colchester's perimeter grew in several directions, but the most significant was the development in the south-west of what became called the New Town area. This was in fact the amalgamation of several building estates, all of which met new and exacting sanitary standards. Such thoroughness was not entirely due to the professionalism of the contractors, sound though they were. In 1877 and 1878 the Borough Council adopted a new and extensive code of by-laws, based on model clauses provided by the Local Government Board under the terms of the 1875 Public Health Act.[17] Prior to this date the Council and its predecessor, the Commissioners, had frequently been frustrated in their attempts to control building standards and to require all new roads and houses to be connected to the main drainage system. Both the law and the Commissioners' Act of Parliament only permitted intervention after an offence had been committed, in other words after a property had been built. Understandably they balked at the draconian remedy of compelling an offending builder to tear down the property he had just erected. From 1878 the new by-laws compelled developers to deposit plans of new houses with the Borough Council. Thereafter the Borough Surveyor could impose strict standards governing the whole process of estate development: the laying out of streets and footpaths, the construction of sewers, the installation of adequate windows, the provision of proper ventilation and drainage and the siting of water closets and ashpits. Before it was inhabited every new property could be checked by the Surveyor's Department to ensure that it met the required standards. Thereafter the keeping of animals (notably pigs), the disposal of rubbish, the conduct of slaughter houses and the destination of industrial waste came under the same official's scrutiny.[18]

The combined consequences of the extended water supply, the new sewers and the improved housing in the 1880s were noted by contemporaries. In 1888 the Medical Officer of Health at Ilfracombe, revising his paper "On the Etiology of Summer Diarrhoea", cast his eye over the national statistics and came across the extraordinary achievements of Colchester. He decided to write to the town:

". . . I find from the Registrar General's quarterly reports that the average death rate from diarrhoea in the third quarters of the eight years 1880-87 is, for the town under your sanitary supervision, some 26 per cent lower than the corresponding average for the ten years 1870-1879, and this holds good *after making full allowance* for the fact that the summer diarrhoea rate for the whole of England and Wales has fallen 2.25 to 2.00 during the same period. Having then, as I believe, eliminated the results of meteorological differences, I should esteem it a very great favour if you would kindly inform me whether there is in your town any change of circumstances to which you would attribute this gratifying result".

There is, of course, no such disease as summer diarrhoea, but it was nonetheless a major source of 19th-century mortality, particularly among infants. It was a classic product of unhygienic domestic surroundings and contaminated food and water, where micro-organisms were rendered doubly virulent by the warm weather of the late summer. According to Victorian dogma, summer diarrhoea was often regarded as a product of teething, a condition considered for much of the century as a disease in its own right. Given that the standard treatment was to administer a powerful emetic (e.g. rhubarb) and to lance the infant's gums – regularly – until the teeth appeared, it was hardly surprising that mortality might result. This barbaric treatment had the added advantage that the profuse bleeding that resulted reduced the pressure of blood upon the skull, thereby containing the risk of convulsions.[19] No wonder that those Victorians who survived childhood were often of a resolute and sturdy disposition.

How far these practices were on the decline in Colchester we do not know, but Colchester's own Medical Officer of Health, Dr Brown, had little doubt as to the reason for the sharp fall in deaths from summer diarrhoea, and incorporated his analysis in his own Annual Report to the Borough Council:

". . . The drainage system has been the chief factor in accomplishing this fortunate condition, by the speedy withdrawal of noxious effete matter from houses, and the ventilation of the surrounding ground and freeing it from soakage; next a free and pure water supply, and the erection of new houses in open and unoccupied spaces as the New Town Field and Lord's Land has prevented the overcrowding of houses – a condition as much to be guarded against as the overcrowding of people – these are the chief causes of this improvement. As a Sanitary Authority it must be a source of much gratification to you to see such results appearing by working out the provisions of the Sanitary Act of 1875, and that you may claim some little credit in this result is undeniable, as it is brought to notice from an independent and unsolicited source".[20]

Faced with such apparent complacency it is salutary to turn to the figures for the 1890s and note that for the first quinquennium the death rate actually rose, albeit by a small amount. This was largely due to two years, 1892 and 1895, which produced respectively the sixth and second largest mortality rates recorded in the century. Part of the blame rested with an influenza epidemic which overwhelmed the local doctors to an extent that had not been known in the town since the cholera outbreak of 1834.[21] But we are also forced to conclude that whatever else had been achieved in Colchester by way of an improved environment and a rising standard of living, the standard of infant care was still in most respects as bad as ever. It is interesting to trace the recognition of this problem in the deliberations of that important figure, the Borough's Medical Officer of Health (M.O.H.), an appointment made first made under the provisions of the 1872 Public Health Act. The growing importance of his work is underlined by the fact that his Annual Report to the Borough Council, beginning as a column in the newspaper had grown by 1900 into a 15-page pamphlet of close print.

Understandably, the Borough's first M.O.H., Dr Edward Waylen, an appointment apparently based on political patronage, concentrated his attentions on environmental factors like nuisance removal, sewage disposal and water supplies, items which, during the 1870s, as we have seen, fully deserved the emphasis they received. Waylen died in 1881, and was briefly succeeded by Dr Finch, whose outcry ten years before against the St. Mary's graveyard we have followed in Chapter Six. Finch and his successor, Dr Brown, began to direct their attention beyond the courts and alleyways to the interiors of the houses that surrounded them. Noting the fact that the infant mortality rate in Colchester was higher than the national average (the death rate was not), Finch declared:

> ". . . the chief fault is to be found in the way young children
> are fed, and to the want of cleanliness . . . if district visitors
> were to make enquiries as to the method of child feeding
> . . . and furnish a few plain rules . . . many lives would be
> saved . . . The chief factors in the diarrhoea of young
> children . . . are to be sought in the emanations from
> neglected dustbins . . . and carelessness about the feed-
> ing bottle. Breast-fed children suffer comparatively
> rarely . . .".[22]

Dr Finch was doubtless reflecting the current campaign of the Local Government Board in favour of breast-feeding, which was based on some disturbing discoveries: that the bulk of cows' milk on sale was adulterated or contaminated or both; that most of it was several days old; that a good deal of it was tubercular; that a host of branded products made from opium were regularly used to silence crying babies; and that where this failed a dummy or a lump of bread was administered, soaked in a sugary mess of water and condensed milk which for days on end was

> "left on the fire hob in a cup, seldom or never changed or cleansed, whence the unfermented and sooty mass is heaped into the infant's mouth".[23]

Much of Colchester's courtyard housing survived into the 20th century. Above, All Saints Court and (left) Market Place, St Peter's Street.

Part of the problem lay in the appalling overcrowding existing in the worst districts of the town, As table 4 shows, the average number of residents per house remained remarkably constant during the period covered by this book.

TABLE 4: Number of Colchester Residents per Inhabited Dwelling in Census Years[24]

1831	:	5.03	1871	:	4.63
1841	:	4.60	1881	:	4.64
1851	:	4.65	1891	:	4.75
1861	:	4.62	1901	:	4.65

Is it significant that the ratio at the 1891 census was marginally the largest? The new brick-built houses of the period 1875-1900 were of course larger than older existing properties, but it is nonetheless hard to argue from these figures that, for all the additional building of this period, the problems of overcrowding had in any way improved. Moreover, an average of 4.75 residents per household included cases of nine people living in two rooms or ten people sleeping in one bedroom.[25] Small wonder that there were regular reports in the press of babies suffocated by their own parents rolling on top of them in their sleep.

Such conditions were not unknown to the mighty of the town whose wives, revolted by the smell or fearful of the attention of fleas and body lice, nonetheless penetrated these swarming tenements in pursuit of charitable exercise. On reflection, it seems, they were more inclined to worry at the moral degeneration that such a total lack of privacy might encourage:

> "Mr Hawkins said . . . his wife happened to be district visitor with, he was happy to say, most of the ladies in St Botolph's parish, and she had called his attention to this case – a man and his wife hired for 1s.6d. a week two rooms which . . . were hardly high enough for a man to stand up in with his hat on, and in addition to the man and his wife there were . . . a daughter aged 20, a daughter aged 18, a daughter aged 14, a boy aged 11, a girl aged 8, a girl aged 5 and a boy aged $1\frac{1}{2}$ . . . he knew of many others as bad . . . What was the use of education, and what was the use of religious education, if children were brought up in that way – what could they look for but demoralisation?"

Public action however, was harder to achieve. For the same laws which entitled a Victorian to regard his home as his castle gave him equal licence to render it a charnel-house. When in 1883 an enthusiastic Liberal councillor wished to arrange for the Corporation's new contractors to collect and empty dustbins on a regular basis, it was John Bawtree Harvey who quietly pointed out that the law did not allow such an invasion of a citizen's privacy until the Sanitary Inspector had formally declared their refuse a 'nuisance'.[26]

Yet it was very clear that the poor, for whom professional medical advice was an unknown luxury, badly needed a crash course in the elements of simple baby care. How might a Public Health Officer intervene in this essentially private act? George Brown, Dr Finch's successor as M.O.H., considered that

> ". . . some simple and easily understandable instructions might be printed and issued by the Sub-Registrar along with the vaccination papers given when the child is registered . . .".[27]

Such a proposal was admirable, but no tangible result followed. As was the case in England as a whole, infant mortality rates in Colchester remained high into the 20th century. The quinquennial average for 1896-1900 was not greatly better than that recorded 50 years before.

TABLE 5: Comparative Quinquennial Infant Mortality Rates[28]

Date	Colchester	England and Wales
1841-45	uncertain	147.4
1846-50	139.8	160.6
1851-55	157.6	156.0
1856-60	152.2	150.2
1861-65	142.4	151.4
1866-70	149.6	156.8
1871-75	137.6	153.2
1876-80	132.3	144.4
1881-85	130.7†	138.6
1886-90	uncertain	145.0
1891-95	146.0†	150.8
1896-00	130.4	156.2
1911-14	78.5	109.5

† *Figures for 1885 and 1891 are unknown.*

Nevertheless the overall death rate did once more significantly fall during this last quinquennium of the century and it is tempting to see in this, as contemporaries did, the beneficial consequences of a "constant supply", finally achieved by James Paxman and the Waterworks Committee.[29] This however was only one factor in a now rising trend towards not just improved public health, but improved private health as well. Crude death rates continued to fall at an impressive rate: 14.5 in 1901-05, 12.6 in 1905-10.

Many factors produced this: improved education, smaller families, milk depots, 'schools' for mothers, maternity grants and that host of legislative initiatives by central government embracing old age pensions, national health insurance, labour exchanges, school meal and medical services, all introduced before the First World War and frequently labelled the 'origins of the Welfare State'. All this lies beyond the scope of this book, but some measure of what was achieved in Colchester can be seen in the infant mortality rate for 1912-14, the last three years before the war. At 68.8 per 1,000 live births this was half the figure that had obtained throughout the reign of Queen Victoria.[30] At long last, it seems, the massacre of the innocent was to abate.

11

Requiescat

Death in the aggregate is only part of the story. One man's statistic is another man's child. For the bulk of Colchester's 19th-century population sapping debility, terminal fevers, premature ageing and regular bereavement were a commonplace of life. For the few, however, life in Victorian Colchester could be as long and as active as it is today. Indeed, in the absence of formal retirement, old age had greater relevance. Born in those insalubrious times before 1840, members of the town's élite might yet enjoy long years with honour. Witnessing as young men the birth of the public health crusade they might yet live to see the inauguration of a constant water supply – or at least glimpse the promised land.

Frederick Blomfield Philbrick, Town Clerk of Colchester at the age of 74, lived to celebrate Queen Victoria's Jubilee, becoming something of a local mascot, having as Town Clerk 50 long years before proclaimed her succession to William IV, when Colchester's cobblestone High Street had echoed to the rattle of the London stage. When he died, aged 81, one son, the Q.C., was Recorder of Colchester, the other, once champion of the Gas Consumers, was a wealthy London solicitor.[1]

John Bawtree Harvey died 18 months before him, full of days and honour, 81 years old, still Chairman of the Gas Company, still Chairman of the Commissioners. Liberal newspapers compared him with Mr Gladstone. His full-page obituary was, appropriately, the largest of the century. It was, they said, the end of an era. In his 'retirement' Harvey compiled scrap-books of press cuttings recording his successes in public life. To those that can read they leave quiet evidence of the complex character of this private public man. His son was a distinguished City banker.[2]

Philbrick and Harvey were predeceased by Henry Jones, a younger man. Death came upon him suddenly. Active and about his work, a blood clot struck him down. He died in the presence of his son-in-law, a Liberal councillor. "I'll meet you", he said, "upon the golden shore".

Henry Jones had a passion for bricks and for controversy. James Paxman thought him one of the most remarkable men of his time. The streets and houses he built still stand in Colchester. The legal practice he established still operates behind the 'new' Town Hall. One son continued the partnership, another became a judge; one daughter married Edwin Sanders, the Chancellor of the Exchequer.[3]

Charles Henry Hawkins also reached his 80s, dying in 1898, 30 years after his brother, 50 years after he himself had been the youngest mayor of Colchester. An indefatigable walker, almost to the last he made the journey across the town he had watched for 75 years to visit his son five miles away at Horkesley. To celebrate his memory his wife presented the clock and Cambridge chimes that sound across Colchester every hour from the tower of the new Town Hall. Remember Charlie Hawkins if you should hear them ring. His political skills passed to his daughter, Dame Catherine Hunt, Colchester's second lady mayor in 1924. How appropriate for the daughter of a man who once said that

> "he trusted they should never have their homes made, what he thought they would be, less happy if the ladies of England had votes . . . because it would be the worst thing that could happen to the women of England to be mixed up with the turmoil of elections".[4]

Peter Bruff continued tirelessly, a legend in his lifetime, endlessly regaling listeners with anecdotes from his past. Active in many enterprises and still Chairman of the Tendring Hundred Waterworks Company, he died aged 87 in 1900 after a full day's work. The great developments that he had planned for Clacton and Frinton were in the end completed by other men. He left an extraordinary will. His best paintings (he had a large collection) he donated to Ipswich. Then in three days of auction his house and his entire estate was sold to finance family annuities. Within four months all trace of him had gone. Few private papers survived; no son stood in his place. One of the most influential figures in East Anglia left no memorial. But if you go to Walton Parish Church there on the chancel wall a pink marble tablet records:

> "To the Glory of God and in loving memory of Peter Schuyler Bruff, Civil Engineer of Ipswich, this East Window is erected by his sorrowing widow and family in Walton, the town he loved so well".[5]

There is no text, but might they not have added Matthew 6.21, "where your treasure is, there will your heart be also"?

James Wicks was the next to go. For him life held a dark conclusion. After the Jumbo controversy his star never rode so high again, even though, against his own party's advice, he stood for Parliament in 1886. Time to some extent mellowed his disposition. He became almost an establishment figure, but never once relented the iron rule of principle. An unbending nonconformist, an unstinting political warrior, perhaps he should have slowed down. His only son, his pride and joy, he inflicted with the christian name, Gladstone. A private school in Cambridge might lead, his father hoped, to university study. It did not. So Gladstone was apprenticed to a printing firm instead, and one Sunday, aged 18, he caught the train to Colchester in company with a lady. James Wicks was doubly scandalised: that his son should travel on a Sunday and be "involved with a girl at his age". The son gave up the relationship, writing "an exquisite letter, admitting his fault". Nine months later he went to a bicycle shop and bought a revolver. Alone, by the beach at Bournemouth, James William Gladstone Wicks put the revolver in his mouth and blew his brains out. In his pocket a book of Swinburne's poems had these words underlined: "I have lived long enough, having seen one thing, and that love hath an end". His father never recovered. Within three years he too was dead. He left no heirs. It was a very Victorian tragedy.[6]

Wilson Marriage and James Paxman lived on into those disturbing days beyond the First World War. To them it was a foreign country. Close friends, they went on business trips abroad, details of which eluded even their families. Paxman lived to 90, Marriage to 89. The Quaker Marriage nearly became a Lord; James Paxman turned down a knighthood. As Lord of the Manor of Stisted, he swopped young men's tales with Judge Philbrick as they walked the partridge woods. At 69 he ran off with Edwin Sanders's daughter. The Chancellor was not pleased. It was a true love match, but nobody believed them. One minor consequence of their elopement was to render vacant the Chairmanship of the Waterworks Committee. It passed, appropriately, to James Wicks for the last sad years of his life. As a schoolboy James Paxman might have seen Fred Philbrick proclaiming Victoria queen, yet he lived to see a world of radio and transatlantic flight. He did not much like motor cars, though his son, Teddy, enjoyed racing at 100 miles per hour. Teddy Paxman was the great grandson of Henry Jones: no wonder he liked furious driving.[7]

Only Jumbo lived to 100, still in 1983 an integral part of the water supply; during the small hours and using cheap electricity, pumped full of water to cope with Colchester's ablutions and breakfast cups of tea. The centenary was suitably celebrated by the Anglian Water Authority, a far more anonymous public body than the beleaguered Borough Council of 100 years before. A reception, an exhibition, a lavish publication – no angry ratepayers asked the reason why. The tense opening ceremony of September 1883 became on 'Jumbo Day' 1983, a people's carnival: abseiling by Boy Scouts down the great tower, charity stalls and a raffle, and genial morris dancing in the mellow autumn sun. Not one note of discord marred the day's events. Admired and respected, the once shocking water-tower was also enjoying an honourable old age.[8]

If all this seemed strange to visiting Victorian ghosts, they had only to seek for the Culver Street Ironworks. A large hole in the ground now marked the site on the proposed Culver Street Development, the subject of a bitter five-year debate still raging in the town. The leader of the Conservative Council had called the scheme a gold mine; his opponents, a sell-out, a rip-off and a sham.[9] Here was an issue that Bawtree Harvey, Fred Philbrick, Henry Jones, the Hawkins brothers, Peter Bruff, James Wicks, Wilson Marriage, James Paxman and John Taylor would all have understood. Let us hope that in 100 years' time historians will as well.

T means the TOP OF THE POLL, and it's found
   That there's many a slip 'twixt the top
    and the ground ;
But who'd not attempt to clamber up there,
When the prize is so great, and the honour so
   rare ?

APPENDIX A: Colchester Birth Rates, Death Rates and Infant Mortality Rates by Year, 1838-1914

YEAR	Adjusted Mid-Year Population	Total Births	Birth Rate	Total Deaths	Death Rate	Deaths Under One Year	Infant Mortality Rate
1838	17,385	U/K	U/K	533	30.7	U/K	U/K
1839	17,547	U/K	U/K	437	24.9	U/K	U/K
1840	17,709	U/K	U/K	488	27.6	U/K	U/K
1838-40					27.7		
1838-42					25.5		
1841	17,790	536	30.1	381	21.4	81	151.1
1842	17,960	576	32.1	417	23.2	102	177.1
1843	18,130	596	32.9	393	21.7	U/K	U/K
1844	18,300	633	34.6	488	26.7	U/K	U/K
1845	18,470	619	33.5	417	22.6	88	142.2
1846	18,640	684	36.7	504	27.0	116	169.6
1847	18,810	604	32.1	500	26.6	98	162.3
1848	18,980	607	32.0	444	23.4	66	108.7
1849	19,150	645	33.7	442	23.1	87	134.9
1850	19,320	656	34.0	388	20.1	81	123.5
1841-45			32.6		23.1		U/K
1846-50			33.7		24.0		139.8
1851	19,490	643	33.0	461	23.7	109	169.5
1852	19,680	626	31.8	474	24.1	108	172.5
1853	19,870	606	30.5	413	20.8	79	130.4
1854	20,060	581	29.0	469	23.4	114	196.2
1855	20,250	604	29.8	432	21.3	72	119.2
1856	22,440	647	28.8	463	20.6	91	140.6
1857	23,130	690	29.8	540	23.3	127	184.1
1858	23,320	721	30.9	503	21.5	91	126.2
1859	23,510	746	31.7	502	21.3	117	156.8
1860	23,690	737	31.2	452	19.1	113	153.3
1851-55			30.8		22.7		157.6
1856-60			30.4		21.1		152.2

YEAR	Adjusted Mid-Year Population	Total Births	Birth Rate	Total Deaths	Death Rate	Deaths Under 1 Year	Infant Mortality Rate
1861	23,890	734	30.8	476	20.0	99	134.8
1862	24,165	754	31.2	453	18.8	91	120.7
1863	24,446	822	33.6	592	24.3	128	155.7
1864	24,699	780	31.6	518	21.0	107	137.2
1865	24,952	843	33.8	540	21.6	138	163.7
1866	25,205	843	33.4	506	20.1	115	136.4
1867	25,458	798	31.3	554	21.8	108	135.3
1868	25,711	784	30.5	461	18.0	108	137.8
1869	25,964	776	29.9	578	22.2	139	179.1
1870	26,217	828	31.6	594	22.7	132	159.4
1861-65			32.2		21.1		142.4
1866-70			31.3		21.0		149.6
1871	26,446	855	32.3	557	21.1	112	131.0
1872	26,648	883	33.1	514	19.3	133	150.6
1873	26,851	860	32.0	505	18.8	111	129.1
1874	27,054	838	31.0	537	19.8	121	144.4
1875	27,257	887	32.6	535	19.8	118	133.0
1876	27,460	885	32.2	501	18.2	114	128.8
1877	27,663	908	32.8	540	19.5	107	117.8
1878	27,866	902	32.4	580	20.8	142	157.4
1879	28,069	897	32.0	538	19.2	113	126.0
1880	28,272	912	32.3	633	22.4	120	131.6
1871-75			32.2		19.7		137.6
1876-80			32.3		20.0		132.3
1881	28,683	928	32.4	487	17.0	119	128.2
1882	29,301	914	31.2	563	19.2	118	129.1
1883	29,919	928	31.0	478	16.0	93	100.2
1884	30,537	901	29.5	575	18.8	149	165.4
1885	31,155	967	31.0	562	18.0	U/K	U/K
1886	31,773	946	29.8	635	20.0	U/K	U/K
1887	32,392	939	29.0	526	16.2	124	132.1
1888	33,011	981	29.7	557	16.9	U/K	U/K

YEAR	Adjusted Mid-Year Population	Total Births	Birth Rate	Total Deaths	Death Rate	Deaths Under One Year	Infant Mortality Rate
1889	33,630	949	28.2	529	15.7	U/K	U/K
1890	34,249	949	27.7	580	16.9	139	146.5
1881-85			31.2		17.8		130.7ᴬ
1886-90			28.9		17.1		U/K
1891	34,749	948	27.3	585	16.8	U/K	U/K
1892	35,130	975	27.8	710	20.2	170	174.4
1893	35,511	1,002	28.2	576	16.3	130	129.7
1894	35,892	995	27.7	476	13.3	93	93.5
1895	36,273	1,035	28.5	721	19.9	193	186.5
1896	36,654	1,005	27.4	515	14.1	134	133.3
1897	37,036	965	26.1	582	15.7	120	124.4
1898	37,418	969	25.9	621	16.6	135	139.3
1899	37,800	985	26.1	600	15.9	133	135.0
1900	38,182	1,000	26.2	604	15.8	120	120.0
1891-95			27.9		17.3		146.0ᴬ
1896-00			26.3		15.6		130.4
1901	38,500	936	24.3	644	16.7	132	141.0
1902	39,008	943	24.2	555	14.2	93	98.6
1903	39,516	1,021	25.8	540	13.7	128	125.4
1904	40,024	1,041	26.0	667	16.7	182	174.8
1905	40,532	1,041	25.7	540	13.3	97	93.5
1906	41,040	975	23.8	539	13.1	125	129.0
1907	41,548	1,009	24.3	517	12.4	84	83.3
1908	42,056	997	23.7	520	12.4	88	88.3
1909	42,564	991	23.3	518	12.2	89	89.8
1910	43,072	948	22.0	551	12.8	87	91.8
1901-05			25.2		14.9		126.7
1906-10			23.4		12.6		96.4

YEAR	Adjusted Mid-Year Population	Total Births	Birth Rate	Total Deaths	Death Rate	Deaths Under One Year	Infant Mortality Rate
1911	43,570[B]	977	22.4[B]	541	12.4[B]	105	107.5
1912	43,970	879	20.0	475	10.8	57	64.8
1913	44,370	885	19.9	499	11.2	53	59.9
1914	44,770	893	19.9	527	11.8	73	81.7
1911-14			20.6		11.6		78.5

U/K = *Unknown.*
A   = *Single Years Missing.*
B   = *Colchester's population was much disrupted by the First World War, and the 1921 census is no guide to pre-war growth. Figures for 1911-14 are therefore very approximate. Working from the net additional births for these years, the author has added an annual figure of 400. This uncertainty renders birth rates and death rates equally approximate.*

SOURCES *Statistics held by the Office of Population Censuses & Surveys, supplemented by the Annual Reports of the M.O.H. for Colchester and figures assembled by the author from the Colchester press.*

Where there are discrepancies between local figures and those supplied by the Office of Population, the latter have in all cases been followed. These discrepancies often occur where births or deaths of those not normally resident in the borough (for example, temporary inmates of the Hospital or Workhouse) have been included or excluded from the totals.

APPENDIX B: Output of the Colchester Waterworks

DATE	Average Weekly Output in gallons	No. of domestic household served	Approximate % of Total Households
1850[A]	c.450,000	{ 640 min { 678 max	15-16%
1858[B]	{ 850,000 min { 1,250,000 max	"not more than 1/3 of the houses" i.e. c.1450	c.30%
1879[C]	2,368,603	3,357	58%
1884[D]	3,140,865	4,481	77%
1889[E]	3,119,858	5,302	81%
1899[F]	c.4,060,000	7,193	89%

Sources:

A. *In a letter of self-defence* (Essex Standard (E.S.) *19/10/1877) Bruff claimed that he had increased the number of Waterworks customers fivefold since 1850. In 1879 the Waterworks served 3,357 households. The total in 1877 would have been less - say 3,200, one fifth of which is 640 (minimum figure).*
Alternatively, both Bruff and Henry Jones agreed that the Waterworks' gross income in 1850 was £700. In 1878-9 it was £4,240, following a 10% increase in the water rate. Deduct the 10% (£424) and an estimated income from the railway contract (£350) and you have a gross figure of £3,466, which is 4.95 times the 1850 income. The same multiplier produces a figure of 678 households in 1850 (maximum figure).

B. *Figures from J. B. Harvey's pamphlet to the Commissioners on the Water Supply dated 8/10/1858 in Harvey Scrapbooks, Local Studies Dept., Colchester Library.*
Alternatively, Bruff in 1859 claimed a weekly output of 1,250,000 gallons: Proceedings of the Institution of Civil Engineering, *Vol 19, pp.38-9.*

C. *Figures from E. Easton's Report on the Colchester Waterworks, dated 24/12/1879 and from a manuscript document prepared for James Paxman entitled "Particulars of Revenue, Quantity of Water Supplied . . . etc." dated 26/11/1889.*

D. *Figures from "Particulars of Revenue . . . etc" dated 26/11/1889 and Annual Report of M.O.H. for 1884 in E.S. 10/2/1885.*

E. *Figures from J. M. Wood: General Report dated 24/4/1890 in Borough of Colchester, Council Summonses, Minutes, etc. 1862-96 in Local Studies Department, Colchester.*

F. *Figures from J. C. Thresh, Report on the Water Supply of the County of Essex (1901), p.137.*

APPENDIX C: Colchester Civilian Population (excluding Garrison)

YEAR	Population	Inter-Censual Increase	% Increase	% Increase England & Wales
1801	11,520	-	-	-
1811	12,544	1,024	8.8	14.3
1821	14,016	1,472	11.7	18.1
1831	16,167	2,151	15.3	15.8
1841	17,790	1,633	10.1	14.5
1851	19,443	1,653	9.3	12.7
1861	20,781	1,338	6.9	11.9
1871	22,867	2,086	10.0	13.2
1881	25,748	2,881	12.6	14.4
1891	30,827	5,079	19.7	11.7
1901	34,452	3,625	11.8	12.2

Sources:
For Colchester: Victoria County History of Essex *Vol II (1907), pp.353-4.*
Contemporary Press Reports: E.S. 26/4/1861, 3/5/1871, 7/5/1881, 19/7/1891, Essex Telegraph 23/4/1901.
For England & Wales: Ryder & Silver, Modern English Society *(1970), p.310.*

X represents the mysterious unknown,
  The magical cross which must never be
  shown ;
And the voter may smile o'er this mystical
  mark
As he thinks of the thousands he keeps in the
  dark.

NOTES & REFERENCES

Common Abbreviations
E.S. - *Essex Standard* (from 1892 *Essex County Standard*); *E.T.* - *Essex Telegraph;* E.R.O. - Essex Record Office; S.R.O. - Suffolk Record Office, Ipswich Branch.; L.S. Col. - Local Studies Library, Colchester (some of this material may subsequently be reclassified); M.W.C. - Borough of Colchester, Minutes of the Waterworks Committee. M.S.C. - Minutes of the Sanitary Committee.

A Note on Newspapers
For most of the period covered by this book Colchester newspapers issued two editions a week. Microfilm collections usually carry only one of these. Thus, in using these footnotes, researchers should check the nearest equivalent date if a given edition appears not to exist. I have also given with each reference the newspaper topic from which it is taken.

Chapter 1 The First Thousand Years
1. For geology see: J.M. Wood, 'Past and Present History of Colchester Waterworks with relation to underground water' in *Essex Naturalist.* Vol 17 (1911), pp.21-36. Also *Essex Standard (E.S.)* 10/8/1848, Letters.
2. *John Norden's Description of Essex, 1594* (1890 Edition), p.18.
3. For the water supply of Roman Colchester see P. Crummy, *Colchester Archaeological Report 3: Excavations at Lion Walk, Balkerne Lane & Middleborough* (1984), pp.26-28.
4. *Morning Chronicle* 6/9/1808, 24/11/1808. See M.R. Hull, *Roman Colchester* (1958), p.242.
5. Dated 15/1/1330 in *Colchester Court Rolls, Vol 1* (1921). Also deeds of 1537 in Local Studies Library, Colchester (L.S.Col.) C.P.L.3. P. Morant, *The History & Antiquities of Colchester* (1748) I, pp.1-2.
6. Deeds and maps in L.S. Col. C.P.L. 47, 48 and 52. Also Morant, *Colchester* I, p.2.
7. Domestic State Papers, Charles I, Vol 418, No.4. *E.S.* 6/10/1883, Letters.
8. *E.S.* 20/10/1883, Letters; L.S. Col., Collection of Local Material by J.B. Harvey (Harvey Scrapbooks), Large Brown Book (L.B.), p.4.
9. Morant, *Colchester* I, p.2.
10. F.W. Robins, *The Story of Water Supply* (1946), p.169.
11. Morant, *Colchester* I, pp.2-3.
12. Morant, *History & Antiquities of the County of Essex* Vol I (1768), p.111.
13. L.S. Col., C.P.L. 115. The original is held by the Colchester and Essex Museum.
14. Essex Record Office (E.R.O.) Q/RUm 1/10; D/DEl Z3; T. Cromwell, *History of Colchester* (1825), pp.301-2; For Dodd see *Dictionary of National Biography.*
15. *East Anglia Postal History Study Circle Bulletin* No.41 (1972), pp.40-1. Water had previously been pumped by an overhead horse mill, driven by bullocks (ex. inf. Dr. Philip Laver).
16. I am indebted to Jim Lee, formerly Engineer to the Colchester Waterworks, for this and other technical explanations.
17. L.S. Col., Harvey Scrapbooks, L.B., p.13.
18. Cromwell, *Colchester,* pp.301-2.
19. Ibid. pp.302-3.
20. *E.S.* 23.1.1857, Commissioners.

21. *E.S.* 17.8.1849, Town Council; Cromwell, *Colchester,* p.192.

Chapter 2 1840-1850: Railways and Public Health
1. See Appendix C. p.155.
2. L.S. Col., Harvey Scrapbooks, Small Brown Book (S.B.). *Ipswich Express (I.E.)* 22.6.1849. See also E.A. Blaxill, *The Street Names of Colchester* (1936) p.27.
3. *E.S.* 22.1.1847, Govt. Enquiry.
4. There is a considerable literature. See S.E. Finer, *The Life and Times of Sir Edwin Chadwick* (1952); R.A. Lewis, *Edwin Chadwick and the Public Health Movement 1832-1854* (1952).
5. *E.S.* 20.4.48, 27.4.48, Meetings.
6. The standard work is D.I. Gordon, *A Regional History of the Railways of Great Britain. Vol. 5 The Eastern Counties* (1968).
7. Ibid p.41.; S. Perry, A letter on the Eastern Counties Railway (1842) (in library of the Essex Archaeological Society); *E.S.* 8.7.1836, Advert.
8. A.F.J. Brown, *Essex People 1750-1900* (1972), pp.167-8. *East Anglia Daily Times (E.A.D.T.)* 26.2.1900, Death of Bruff.
9. Gordon, *Eastern Counties,* pp.28, 68-9; H.F. Hilton, *The Eastern Union Railway* (1946), pp.8-10.
10. *E.A.D.T.* 26.2.1900, 2.3.1900, Death of Bruff. For the Schuylers see *Dictionary of American Biography.*
11. *E.S.* 11.6.1846, Report; 20.6.1846, Letters; 27.6.1846, Borough Court; 2.1.1863, Tendring Hundred Railway; R. Malster, *Ipswich, Town on the Orwell* (1978), pp.93-96.; Hilton, *Eastern Union,* pp.13-14.
12. *E.S.* 23.12.1842, Letters; 19.4.1844, Public Meeting; 10.5.1844, Commissioners.
13. *E.S.* 17.1.1840, Colchester; 5.2.1847, Govt. Enquiry.
14. *E.S.* 8.11.1850, Stour Valley Railway; Gordon, *Eastern Counties,* p.154.
15. *E.S.* 7.11.1846, 14.11.1846, Leader and Commissioners. These events are well discussed in A.F.J. Brown, *Colchester 1815-1914* (1980), pp.16-18.
16. Gordon, *Eastern Counties,* pp.28-29.
17. Ibid. p.96; Hilton, *Eastern Union,* pp.19-24, 27-32.
18. Gordon, *Eastern Counties,* pp.154-7; *E.S.* 23.4.1847, 17.5.1861, Railway Enquiries.
19. *E.S.* 22.1.1847, Govt. Enquiry; 12.3.1847, Colchester.
20. *E.S.* 24.9.1847, Commissioners; 7.5.1852, 14.5.1852, Leader.
21. *E.S.* 22.1.1847, Enquiry; 16.7.1847 Letters; 7.5.1856, 8.10.1856, 14.11.1856, 6.5.1857, 9.9.1857, 7.3.1860, Commissioners.
22.*E.S.* 22.1.1847, Enquiry.
23. *E.S.* 23.7.1852, 22.7.1853, Mechi Gathering; 9.3.1864, 5.9.1866, Commissioners; Finer, *Chadwick,* p.300; Mechi, *How to Farm Profitably* (1864), pp.100-106, 530-552.
24. *E.S.* 5.7.1854, 6.7.1855, 3.10.1860, Commissioners; 30.4.1847, Advert; F.B. Smith, *The People's Health 1830-1910* (1979), p.220.
25. *E.S.* 5.7.1854, Commissioners; 7.7.1848, Advert; 28.8.1849, Inquest.
26. E.R.O. D/DEl Z3; *E.S.* 20.7.1849, Letters; *Ipswich Express (I.E.)* 3.7.1849, Letter; 31.7.1849, Colchester Water; undated editorial in L.S. Col., Harvey Scrapbooks, S.B; Appendix B p.154; For the problems experienced by the Hospital in dealing with the Waterworks Company, see J.B. Penfold: *The History of the Essex County Hospital, Colchester, 1820-1948* (1984) p.42.
27. K.S. Inglis, 'Patterns of Religious Worship in 1851' in *Journal of Ecclesiastical History* Vol. 11, No.1 (April 1960); A. Phillips, 'Mormons in Essex 1850-1870' in *Essex Journal* Vol.18 No.3 (1983) p.58.
28. *Essex Telegraph (E.T.)* 16.8.1890, Harvey Obit.
29. *E.S.* 5.11.1847, Election Results; 11.8.1848, Editorial; *E.T.* 31.10.1885, Meeting Third Ward.
30. *E.S.* 13.7.1849, 20.7.1849, 27.7.1849, 31.7.1849, 10.8.1849, Letters; Poster of 1849 in the possession of the Anglian Water Authority; *I.E.* 28.8.1849, Editorial.
31. *I.E.* 31.7.1849, 7.8.1849 in L.S. Col., Harvey Scrapbooks.
32. Finer, *Chadwick,* pp.220-1, 297-8, 319; G. Rosen, 'Disease, Debility and Death' in H.J. Dyos & M. Wolff (eds.), *The Victorian City, Images and Realities* (1973), pp.635-6.
33. Finer, *Chadwick* p.347; Smith, *The People's Health,* p.232.

34. Finer, *Chadwick*, pp.336-7; *E.S.* 5.1.1849, Commissioners; 12.1.1849, Colchester.
35. Finer, *Chadwick* p.347; *E.S.* 21.9.1849, 12.10.1849, Town Council.
36. *E.S.* 19.10.1849, Commissioners; 11.1.1850, Town Council.
37. *E.S.* 9.2.1849, Commissioners; 17.5.1850, Town Council; 24.5.1850, Great Exhibition.
38. *E.S.* 25.1.1850, 5.7.1850, Commissioners.
39. *E.S.* 3.5.1850, Guardians; 7.6.1850, 5.7.1850, Commissioners.
40. *E.S.* 24.1.1851, Colchester.

Chapter 3 1850-1860: Mr Harvey Proposes
1. White's *Directory of Essex, 1863* p.74; *E.S.* 7.3.1851, Letters.
2. *E.S.* 23.4.1847, Railway Intelligence; 30.4.1847, Shareholders; 18.6.1847, Stour Valley; Hilton, *Eastern Union*, pp.4, 43.
3. Gordon, *Eastern Counties* p.154; *E.S.* 1.9.1848, 2.3.1849, Stour Valley.
4. *E.S.* 17.11.1848, Stour Valley; 23.2.1861, Carr v. Directors; Suffolk Record Office (S.R.O.) HC 14 BL 2885 letters pp.20-21. See also the squib 'Twelve Naughty Boys' in L.S. Col., Harvey Scrapbooks.
5. *E.S.* 13.10.1848, Meeting Shareholders.
6. *E.S.* 6.7.1849, E. Union; Minutes of the Proceedings of the Institution of Civil Engineers (P.Inst.C.E.) Vol. 9. (1850), pp.292-3.
7. *E.S.* 1.9.1848, 17.11.1848, 24.11.1848, Colchester.
8. *E.S.* 4.5.1849, Investigation; 11.5.1849, Shareholders. On Hudson see R.S. Lambert, *The Railway King, 1800-1871. A study of George Hudson and the Business Morals of his Time* (1934).
9. *E.S.* 10.5 1850, Timetable; 11.6.1847, Parl Committee; Gordon, *Eastern Counties*, p.69. The delays on the London-Colchester-Ipswich line prompted several drolleries in *Punch* such as the 16-year-old boy arrested at Ipswich for travelling on a child's ticket who claimed in his defence that he had been 12 years old when the train had left London.
10. S.R.O., HC 14 BL 2885, letters dated 29.4.1850, 13.9.1850, 10.10.1850; *E.S.* 19.10.1849, Commissioners.
11. S.R.O. HC 14 BL 2885 letters 2.11.1851, 2.12.1851, 13.1.1852; Wood, *History of Colchester Waterworks.*
12. *E.S.* 22.12.1854, 19.1.1855, Catchpool v. Cooper; 4.2.1859, Chelmsford; *Essex and West Suffolk Gazette (E.W.S.G.)* 19.1.1855; Whitaker and Thresh, *Water Supply of Essex* (1916), p.127; P.Inst.C.E. Vol.19 (1859), pp.38-9.
13. Wood, *History of Colchester Waterworks;* E.S. 10.6.1853, Commissioners; L.S. Col., Harvey Scrapbooks, 1858 Report to the Commissioners on the Water Supply (Harvey 1858 Report).
14. *E.S.* 5.7.1854, 8.9.1854, Commissioners.
15. *E.S.* 6.7.1855, 9.11.1855, 9.4.1856, 7.10.1857, 4.11.1857, 18.11.1857, Commissioners; 4.6.1875, Rating Enquiry.
16. *E.S.* 9.2.1859, 6.4.1859, 6.5.1859, Commissioners: Harvey 1858 Report.
17. Ibid; *E.S.* 12.9.1865, Commissioners.
18. Harvey 1858 Report; *E.S.* 9.2.1859.

Chapter 4 1860-1870: Mr Bruff Declines
1. *E.S.* 3.11.1858, Commissioners; 13.5.1859, Colchester.
2. *E.S.* 18.4.1851, Census; 6.12.1861, Clerical Conference.
3. Gordon, *Eastern Counties*, pp.69, 74; *E.S.* 3.12.1859, Bruff v. E. Counties.
4. Ibid.; *E.S.* 18.1.1856, 1.2.1856, 14.3.1856, E. Counties; 14.1.1857, Letters.
5. S.R.O. HC 14 BL 2885 Letter 27.10.1856; E.S. 3.12.1858, Bruff v. E. Counties; 1.5.1874, Bruff v. E. Union.
6. J. Leather, *The Northseamen* (1971), p.270; S.R.O. HC 14 BL 2885 loose papers.
7. *E.S.* 16.12.1857, Colchester; S.R.O. HC 14 BL 2885 letters 11.12.1857 ff.
8. S.R.O. HC 14 BL 2889 letters.
9. L. Weaver, *The Harwich Story* (1975), pp.134, 122-3; S.R.O. HC 14 BL 2885; P.Inst.C.E. Vol.19 (1859), pp.39-40; *E.T.* 21.4.1883, Tendring Water; *E.A.D.T.*

26.2.1900, Death of Bruff.
10. For Walton see T. Wilmshurst, *A Descriptive Account of Walton-on-the-Naze* (1860);
P.B. Boyden, *Walton 1800-1867* (1981).
11. *E.S.* 7.9.1866, 22.9.1876, 4.11.1882, Letters; L.S. Col., Gazette Guide to Walton-
on-the-Naze (1887).
12. E.R.O. D/P 229/24/3; *E.S.* 25.6.1841, 16.7.1841, 6.8.1841, 26.9.1841, Colchester;
Boyden, *Walton*, pp.14-22.
13. F. Hussey, *The Royal Harwich* (1972), p.39; *E.A.D.T.* 26.2.1900, Death of Bruff;
Ipswich Journal 4.5.1833, Advert; *E.S.* 4.8.1871, Clacton; 29.3.1890, Walton Defences;
4.11.1882, Letters; E.R.O. D/DB T189 Deeds. Bruff did not of course originate the idea
of a railway to Walton: *E.S.* 25.6.1841, Colchester.
14. *E.S.* 29.9.1858, Colchester; 8.7.1859, Parl. Enquiry; 14.3.1862, 12.12.1862,
Tendring Railway; S.R.O. HC 14 BL 2885 letter 29.12.1861.
15. *E.S.* 8.7.1859, Parl. Enquiry; 14.3.1862, Tendring Railway; 24.12.1862, Letters.
16. *E.S.* 14.3.1862, Colchester; 5.5.1865, 9.6.1865, Commissioners. William Hawkins
briefly returned to the district in about 1903, when he was seen, complete with his stick,
climbing over the pews in his parish church at Alresford. An official church ceremony
was required to pacify his troubled spirit. What did he have on his mind? (ex. inf. D.
Cardy).
17. *E.S.* 6.5.1863, 23.3.1866, 6.4.1866, 17.5.1867, 17.7.1867, 29.11.1867, Tendring
Railway; 12.2.1868, Death of Hawkins.
18. *E.S.* 17.8.1859, 17.2.1860, 7.11.1862, 29.3.1890, Walton; 18.11.1865, Advert;
Wilmshurst, *Walton;* White's *Directory of Essex 1863;* S.R.O. HC 14 BL 2885 letters
10.7.1862, and 3176/44 Walton Pier; K. Walker, *The History of Clacton* (1966), p.30;
E.R.O. Q/RUm/2/153; 1861 Census, Enumerators' Returns.
19. *E.T.* 11.3.1881, Harwich Water; 21.4.1883, Tendring Water; *E.A.D.T.* 26.2.1900,
Death of Bruff; T. Miller, *Harwich Harbour* (1926), pp.1-13; B.C. Hughes, *The History
of Harwich Harbour* (1939), pp.32-65.
20. Brown, *Colchester*, pp.167-8; Smith, *The People's Health*, pp.216-7; *E.S.* 7.8.1863,
Town Council; 7.1.1863, Colchester; 9.11.1866, Letters.
21. *E.S.* 8.5.1861, 5.6.1861, 3.7.1861, 12.9.1865, 6.10.1865, 8.12.1865, Commissioners.
22. *E.S.* 9.2.1866, Commissioners; 16.3.1866, Colchester; 29.7.1868, 6.10.1869,
Commissioners.
23. *E.S.* 9.11.1866, Registrar General; 3.7.1867, Commissioners.

Chapter 5 1870-1878: Seasides and Gasworks

1. See Chapter 10, pp.130-145.
2. Gordon, *Eastern Counties*, pp.31-2; E.R.O. Q/RUm/2/150; *E.S.* 15.5.1868, Tendring
Railway.
3. S.R.O. HC 14 3176/20 Walton Station. Compare the illustrations in L.S. Col., 'Views
of Walton 1871' and Dorling's *Guide to Walton* (1878).
4. *E.S.* 18.2.1870, Walton Commissioners; 1.3.1878, Gas etc., Walton; 22.3.1879,
Walton.
5. *E.S.* 18.11.1865, Advert; 4.9.1880, Clacton Station; *E.W.S.G.*, 28.4.1871, Advert.
For the development of Clacton see J. Skudder, 'The Seaside Resort as a Business
Venture (Clacton-on-Sea 1864-1901)', University of Essex B.A. Thesis (1980).
6. *E.S.* 25.11.1870, Colchester; 2.12.1870, 9.12.1870, Letters.
7. *E.S.* 28.7.1871, 4.8.1871, Clacton; *Kentish Independent* 29.7.1871.
8. Ibid.; E.R.O. D/DOp B103; Skudder, *The Seaside Resort.*
9. Ibid.; *E.S.* 4.10.1879, 15.11.1879, Clacton; *E.A.D.T.* 26.2.1900, Death of Bruff.
10. *E.S.* 3.1.1866, 8.6.1870, 6.3.1872, Commissioners; 25.8.1876, Waterworks;
6.4.1877, 27.12.1879, Town Council.
11. M. Falkus, 'Development of Municipal Trading in the Nineteenth Century' in
Business History Vol.19 (1977); R. Grinter, *Joseph Chamberlain: Democrat, Unionist and
Imperialist* (1971), p.11. A classic study of Birmingham is in Asa Briggs, *Victorian Cities*
(1963), Chapter 5.
12. Cromwell, *Colchester*, p.306; J.B. Harvey, *Gas Lighting in Colchester* (1890), pp.3-7;

E.S. 20.4.1838, Advert.; 16.2.1849, Colchester; 23.2.1849, Advert.; 19.4.1850, Court of Bankruptcy; 23.2.1866, Commissioners; L.S., Col., Harvey Scrapbooks, S.B., cutting 19.8.1848

13. *E.T.* 30.1.1866, Letter; 14.11.1865, Advert.; E.R.O. D/F 27/2/2, 26.5.1865, 15.11.1865, 17.11.1865.

14. *E.S.* 6.2.1892, Philbrick obit.; Hughes, *Harwich Harbour*, p.197; H.J. Hanham, *Elections and Party Management: Politics in the time of Gladstone & Disraeli* (1959), p.237; E.R.O. D/F 27/2/3, Frontispiece. On Philbrick's pique see a revealing correspondence in L.S. Col., Rebow Papers, John Gurdon Rebow Correspondence.

15. E.R.O. D/F 27/2/2, 8.1.1866, 12.2.1866; *E.S.* 7.5.1875, Parl. Examination. In fact, the Army was the Gas Company's best customer.

16. E.R.O. D/F 27/2]2, 15.2.1866, 25.6.1866; *E.T.* 23.1.1866, 6.2.1866, Letters; *E.S.* 23.2.1866, 18.5.1866, Commissioners; Harvey, *Gas in Colchester*, p.9.

17. *E.S.* 4.5.1866, Letters; *E.T.* 22.5.1866, Letters.

18. Ibid.; *E.S.* 9.5.1866, 6.6.1866, 4.7.1866, Commissioners; 1.6.1866, 8.8.1866, 13.2.1867, Letters; 28.12.1866, Leader; 24.4.1867, Taylor Obit.

19. *E.S.* 3.1.1872, 7.2.1872, 8.3.1872, 5.4.1872, 10.5.1872, Commissioners.

20. Harvey, *Gas in Colchester*, p.10; *E.S.* 24.6.1874, Gas Company; 4.12.1874, Town Council; 27.1.1875, Public Meeting.

21. *E.S.* 24.9.1847, 27.4.1848, 7.6.1850, 14.6.1850, 19.7.1850, 6.12.1850, Court Cases; 22.10.1852, Colchester; 26.10.1889, Jones Obit.; 16.11.1889, Letter.

22. *E.S.* 4.12.1874, Town Council; 1.1.1875, 15.1.1875, 27.1.1875, Public Meetings.

23. E.R.O. D/F 27/2/4, 9.7.1874, 27.7.1874, 17.12.1874; Harvey, *Gas in Colchester*, pp.11-12.

24. Ibid.; *E.S.* 19.3.1875, 7.5.1875, Gas Bill; 9.4.1875, 16.4.1875, Town Council.

25. *E.S.* 25.6.1875, Gas A.G.M.; 2.7.1875, Letters; 3.10.1866, Harvey Presentation; Manuscript book entitled 'History of Nonconformity; J.B. Harvey' now in the possession of Mr. John Bensusan-Butt.

26. L.S. Col., Harvey Scrapbooks, S.B., cutting 30.4.1846.

27. E.S. 1.1.1875, Public Meeting.

Chapter 6 1870-1878: Graveyards and Fires

1. For fires see *E.S.* 17.12.1852, 10.5.1867, 10.12.1873. There is a comprehensive list in L.S. Col., Harvey Scrapbooks.

2. *E.S.* 5.3.1847, Letter; 16.1.1874, Commissioners; 29.3.1878, Letters.

3. *E.S.* 16.1.1874, Commissioners; 8.5.1874, 9.2.1877, 6.4.1877, Town Council; 30.11.1877, 18.1.1878, Colchester; Colchester Borough Council, Minutes of Sanitary Committee (M.S.C.), 26.1.1876, 7.2.1876.

4. *E.S.* 22.2.1878, Fire and Letters; 8.3.1878, Colchester; 22.3.1878, Letter.

5. *E.S.* 3.1.1866, Commissioners; 16.1.1874, 8.3.1878, Town Council.

6. *E.S.* 8.9.1865, Commissioners; 13.10.1865, Doctors' Report; See also Chapter 10, Table 1: p.131.

7. *E.S.* 10.5.1872, Guardians. On the changing status of the Victorian G.P. see Smith, *People's Health*, pp.362-382.

8. C.E. Benham, *Colchester Worthies* (1892), p.10; *E.S.* 20.12.1872, Colchester; 10.5.1872, 22.5.1872, Guardians; 5.6.1872, Commissioners.

9. *E.S.* 6.6.1872, County Magistrates; 12.6.1872, Brightlingsea; Smith, *People's Health*, pp.160-170.

10. Ibid. pp.166-8; *E.S.* 25.4.1873, Ag. Labourers Union; 21.11.1873, 27.2.1874, 6.5.1874, 11.9.1874, 30.10.1874, 11.12.1874, 16.4.1875, Court Cases. John Castle of Coggeshall should not be confused with his relative, John Castle of Colchester, a founder of the Colchester Co-operative Society.

11. *E.S.* 5.6.1872, Court Case.

12. *E.S.* 10.5.1872, Guardians; 10.9.1881, 24.12.1881, 10.5.1884, Town Council.

13. For the story that follows see *E.S.* 18.8.1871, St. Mary's Enquiry; 6.9.1871, Commissioners.

14. A.S. Wohl, *Endangered Lives: Public Health in Victorian Britain* (1983), pp.95-98; B. Barber, 'Municipal Government in Leeds 1835-1914' in D. Fraser (Ed.), *Municipal Reform & the Industrial City* (1982), p.69.

15. *E.S.* 8.9.1858, 11.6.1862, 7.8.1863, 7.10.1863, Commissioners; 9.11.1866, Letters; 3.6.1874, Leader; 18.1.1879, County Court; 4.6.1881, Letter.
16. *E.S.* 18.8.1871, Sanitary Enquiry; 12.9.1865, 6.10.1865, Commissioners; 1.1.1875, Public Meeting; 16.2.1877, 25.9.1886, Colchester.
17. *E.S.* 30.4.1875, 30.3.1877, Letters; M.S.C. 6.4.1875.
18. *E.S.* 3.9.1875, 8.10.1875, Town Council. See also M.S.C. for this period.
19. *E.T.* 23.10.1866; E.S. 14.7.1858, Colchester; 6.11.1867, County Court; 5.4.1878, 5.7.1879, Town Council; 15.2.1878, Court Case; Also relevant M.S.C.
20. *E.S.* 5.1.1877, Town Council.
21. *E.S.* 16.3.1877, Town Council; 8.3.1878, Letter.
22. E.S. 5.4.1878, Town Council; 6.7.1878, Colchester; Wohl, *Endangered Lives*, pp.249-50.

Chapter 7 1878-1880: Municipal Purchase

1. E.S. 10.11.1876, Mayor Making; 12.1.1877, Court Case; 31.1.1877, Law Lords; 8.6.1877, 13.7.1877, 3.8.1877, Town Council; *E.T.* 4.5.1877, Town Council.
2. . . and did not detain its users long either. Public indignation at the desecration of consecrated walls soon forced its closure. E.S. 8.3.1871, Commissioners.
3. J.S. Appleby and P.A. Watkinson, *The Parish Church of St Runwald, Colchester* (1942), p.20; *Colchester, Official Guide* (4th Ed. 1973), p.51.
4. *E.S.* 8.3.1878, 7.9.1878, Town Council; E.R.O., D/DEl Z3.
5. Ibid.; White's *Directory of Essex, 1848; E.S.* 8.3.1878, Town Council; 26.10.1889, Jones Obit.
6. *E.S.* 8.3.1878, Town Council; L.S. Col., Colchester Corporation Letter Book (C.L.B.), 21.2.1878, 25.2.1878, 26.2.1878.
7. Falkus, 'Development of Municipal Trading', op. cit.; *E.S.* 19.10.1877, Letter; 8.3.1878, Town Council; M.S.C., 7.2.1876, 11.4.1877.
8. Minutes of the Colchester Water Supply Committee, later the Waterworks Committee (M.W.C.), 11.10.1880, 15.1.1883; E.S. 25.8.1876, Waterworks A.G.M.
9. *E.A.D.T.* 26.2.1900, Bruff Obit; *E.S.* 30.11.1877, 1.3.1878, 8.3.1878, Walton Commissioners.
10. *C.L.B.* 22.3.1878, 24.4.1878; *E.S.* 7.9.1878, 7.12.1878, Town Council; 16.11.1878, Advert.; 8.3.1879, Public Meeting.
11. *E.S.* 18.1.1879, County Court.
12. *E.S.* 8.3.1879, 15.3.1879, Public Meetings; 22.3.1879, 5.4.1879, 19.4.1879, Town Council; M.W.C., 4.3.1879, 15.3.1879.
13. *C.L.B.* 17.7.1879, *E.S.* 6.9.1879, Waterworks Enquiry; 7.12.1878, 27.12.1879, Town Council; 8.3.1879, 15.3.1879, Public Meetings; 22.3.1879, 19.4.1879, Town Council.
14. Borough of Colchester, *Centenary of Municipal Corporation Act 1835* (1936), pp.7-9, 46; *Essex & Suffolk Times* 5.1.1838; *E.S.* 24.11.1837, Colchester; 16.11.1878, Mayor Making.
15. E.S. 6.1.1860, Meeting, Volunteers; 13.11.1861, Mayor Making; 17.11.1865, 3.8.1877, Town Council; 9.10.1872, Colchester; 18.10.1872, 30.10.1872, 1.11.1872, Leader and Elections; 23.10.1872, Oyster Feast.
16. *E.S.* 24.3.1875, Public Meeting; 20.1.1875, 12.2.1875, 14.4.1875, 16.6.1875, 23.6.1875, 29.12.1875, 3.5.1876, 7.1.1882, 14.1.1882, Guardians.
17. *E.S.* 15.11.1879, Mayor Making; 7.1.1880, Town Council; 22.3.1867, Parl. Examination; *E.T.* 4.11.1879, Liberal Meeting.
18. *E.S.* 9.8.1878, 15.11.1879, 7.2.1880, 10.4.1880, Town Council; 24.4.1880, Tendring Railway; 29.9.1883, Watertower Opening; Falkus, 'Development of Municipal Trading'.
19. *E.S.* 6.3.1880, 10.4.1880, 8.5.1880, 26.6.1880, 28.8.1880, Town Council; *E.T.* 30.4.1880, Leader and Bill of Costs.
20. *E.S.* 26.6.1880, Town Council; 3.11.1883, 10.11.1883, 17.11.1883, Letters; M.W.C., 27.10.1880; *C.L.B.* 14.4.1880. The missing deeds were never found.
21. *E.S.* 9.8.1879, 27.12.1879, Town Council; M.W.C. 1.12.1879.
22. Opinions of Mr Jim Lee and Mr John Mitchell; *E.S.* 10.11.1883, 17.11.1883,

Letters; 9.7.1892, Town Council; Letter from J.M. Wood to the Waterworks Committee, dated 23.9.1907, in the possession of the Anglian Water Authority.
23. *E.S.* 3.1.1880, Advert.; 3.11.1883, Letter; M.W.C. 3.2.1880, 11.10.1880, 27.10.1800. These financial manoeuvres were not all plain sailing. There is a ring of déjà vu about the entry of 25.1.1886: 'future payments of interest on Indenture No. 21 to be withheld until questions pending between Mr W. Tindall, Mr P.S. Bruff and the Union Bank of London as to the ownership of the mortgage has been decided.'
24. M.W.C. 27.10.1880, 10.1.1881, 27,9.1886.

Chapter 8 1880-1885: Municipal Tribulation

1. For example, by 1885 the Liberals were able to claim a 58% increase in the hours of supply and a daily provision of 30 gallons per head of population. This compares favourably with a national survey of 1888 which gave figures ranging from 8 gallons a day at Oldham to 25 at Preston among our major cities. *E.S.* 19.9.1885, Enquiry; 10.10.1885, Town Council; Fraser and Sutcliffe (eds.), *The Pursuit of Urban History* (1983), p.230.
2. M.W.C. 22.11.1880, 29.11.1880, 31.1.1881, 10.1.1881, 26.9.1881.
3. M.W.C. 10.1.1881, 29.8.1881, *E.S.* 3.1.1866, 6.5.1874, Commissioners.
4. Best summarized in J.H. Round, *History & Antiquities of Colchester Castle* (1882), p.3.
5. *E.S.* 2.4.1881, 9.4.1881, Town Council. An earlier estimate made Colchester the third largest borough after Warwick and Tiverton, *E.S.* 13.9.1867.
6. R. Grinter, *Joseph Chamberlain*, pp.15-16. It is a nice irony that these words were directed at the Marquis of Salisbury, Chamberlain's future Unionist colleague.
7. *E.S.* 9.4.1881, 10.12.1881, Town Council; M.W.C. 29.8.1881.
8. *E.S.* 27.5.1882, Watertower; M.W.C. 29.8.1881, 20.3.1882.
9. See M.W.C. for 1881-82.
10. M.W.C. 19.8.1882; *E.S.* 28.10.1882, Colchester. Everetts still hold a fine run of 19th-century letter books, but through the operation of a law, well known to us all, the volumes covering the construction of the Watertower are missing.
11. M.W.C. 10.1.1881, 23.3.1885, 23.5.1887; *E.S.* 9.7.1881, Town Council. 15.9.1883, Enquiry; Posters held by the Anglian Water Authority.
12. M.W.C. 20.3.1882, 10.1.1883, 15.1.1883, 28.5.1883, 29.10.1883; *E.S.* 12.5.1883, Town Council.
13. M.W.C. 3.2.1880, 11.10.1880; *E.S.* 13.11.1880, Mayor Making; *E.T.* 22.9.1888, Men We All Know.
14. *E.S.* 1.5.1880, Colchester; 20.5.1882, Letter; 29.9.1883, Watertower; M.W.C. 24.4.1882, 15.5.1882.
15. *E.S.* 3.6.1882, 15.9.1883, Poems; 5.5.1883, Leader; *E.T.* 29.12.1883, Theatre.
16. M.W.C. 21.5.1883, 23.7.1883, 20.8.1883.
17. *E.S.* 15.9.1883, Enquiry.
18. M.W.C. 27.8.1883; *E.S.* 3.11.1883, Letter.
19. *E.S.* 29.9.1883, Watertower Opening; On Rawlinson see: G.M. Binnie, *Early Victorian Water Engineers* (1981), Chapter 10 and Finer, *Life of Chadwick*, pp.299-300, 446, 511-2.
20. *E.S.* 23.2.1877, 17.8.1877, 25.2.1882, 25.8.1883, 16.2.1889, Gas Company; Harvey, *Gas in Colchester*, pp.13,18,21.
21. Falkus, 'Development of Municipal Trading', op. cit.

Chapter 9 1885-1895: Civic Responsibilities

1. *E.S.* 3.11.1883, 10.11.1883, 17.11.1883, 1.12.1883, 8.12.1883, Letters; 13.11.1883, 4.7.1885, Colchester Jottings.
2. *E.S.* 17.11.1883, Letter; M.W.C. 19.11.1883.
3. *E.S.* 5.7.1884, 4.7.1885, Town Council; 13.6.1885, Leader; M.W.C. 28.1.1884.
4. *E.S.* 8.11.1884, Municipal Elections; 5.5.1888, Town Council; 8.11.1890, Poem.
5. *E.S.* 24.10.1885, Election Address and Political Rallies; 14.11.1885, Mayor making. For an example of 'personalities' see *E.S.* 9.10.1886, 23.10.1886, Town Council.
6. *E.T.* 5.8.1885, Mayor's Meeting; 10.9.1885, 13.2.1886, Leader; *E.S.* 23.4.1887, Leader, Town Council and St. Nicholas Easter Tea; 1.10.1887, Leader; 9.5.1885, 26.9.1885, 19.11.1887, 4.2.1888, Town Council; 27.10.1888, Leader.

7. *E.S.* 10.3.1888, Unionist Rally.
8. M.W.C. 15.10.1883, 12.11.1883, 19.5.1884, 16.6.1884, 20.7.1884, 23.5.1887; *E.S.* 17.11.1883, Town Council; letters written by C.E. Bland, Waterworks Superintendent, now held by the Anglian Water Authority.
9. See Appendix B p.154. These calculations are based on J.M. Wood's 'General Report', dated 24.4.1890 in L.S. Col., Council Summonses, Minutes & Committee Minutes 1862-96 and 'Particulars of Revenue, Quantity of Water Supplied . . . etc.', dated 26.11.1889, one of several relevant manuscript documents in E.R.O. Paxman Papers (unclassified at the time of writing). See also *E.S.* 15.9.1883, 19.9.1885, Enquiry; M.W.C. 30.6.1885, 2.1.1886.
10. For Wood's Reports see L.S. Col., Council Summonses etc. 1862-96. *E.S.* 29.9.1883, Watertower Opening; 7.12.1889, Town Council; M.W.C. 28.4.1884, 28.4.1886. During the earthquake Jumbo was seen to sway from side to side.
11. A copy of Wood's 'General Report', now in the possession of Mr Jim Lee, carries the handwritten comment: "Mr Wood's recommendation was not carried out. Mr Paxman opposed the lowering of the well shaft to 93 feet – an awful mistake. C.E. Bland."; *E.S.* 19.9.1895, Lexden Enquiry.
12. *E.S.* 6.9.1879, 15.9.1883, Enquiry; 10.10.1885, Town Council; 8.8.1885, Leader; E. Easton, Report, dated 24.12.1889; 'Particulars of Revenue etc . . ., dated 26.11.1889 and 'Particulars asked for by . . . Mr Paxman', dated 3.12.1889 in E.R.O. Paxman Papers (unclassified).
13. *E.S.* 2.12.1882, 7.4.1883, 22.11.1884, 5.2.1887, Town Council; 28.10.1882, Free Library; 5.1.1884, Editorial; 14.6.1884, Electric Light; 28.3.1885, School of Art; 1.1.1887, Letter; 19.2.1887, Public Meeting; 11.6.1887, Tramway Advert.; L.S. Col. Borough of Colchester, Abstract of Accounts 1907-8 p.238.
14. *E.S.* 2.8.1884, Sewage Works; 4.10.1884, Town Council.
15. Ibid.; *E.S.* 26.7.1884, 9.8.1884, Letter; 6.12.1884, Commissioners; 4.7.1885, 8.10.1887, Town Council; 7.11.1885, Municipal Election.
16. *E.S.* 27.10.1888, Leader; 26.10.1889, Letters; 24.11.1888, Second Ward Vacancy; *E.T.* 8.11.1890, Municipal Election; *E.S.* 8.11.1890, Poem. Note the affectation, which did not long survive, of placing T.C. (Town Councillor) after councillors' names in the press *E.T.* 5.5.1879.
17. L.S. Col., Town Council Reports 1879-80, 1889-90.
18. *E.S.* 1.10.1887, Leader; 22.10.1887, 27.10.1888, 22.10.1892, Oyster Feasts; 30.6.1888, Letters; 19.3.1887, Railway Dinner; 18.6.1887, Standard Iron Celebration.
19. L.S. Col. Harvey Scrapbooks, 1858 Report.
20. Colchester's rateable value rose from £45,000 in 1837 to £77,000 in 1870 and £140,800 in 1896. *E.S.* 28.2.1872, Town Council; Benham's *Guide to Colchester, 1897*, p.20.
21. *E.S.* 21.4.1883, 15.9.1883, 16.2.1884, Hospital; 20.10.1894, Library; 10.12.1898, Hawkins Obit.; 7.3.1885, Recreation ground; 7.4.1883, Town Council; 27.9.1872, Colchester; 20.12.1872, Education Question; 25.2.1888, New Town School.
22. James Paxman is a good example. See M.W.C. 29.8.1881 and *E.S.* 27.10.1888, Oyster Feast. For the Oyster Feast: D. Cannadine, 'The transformation of Civic Ritual in Modern Britain: The Colchester Oyster Feast' in *Past & Present* No.94 (1982).
23. *E.S.* 27.7.1889, Soldiers Home; 26.10.1892, Castle Park; 24.10.1896, Albert School; 23.7.1932, Marriage Obit.
24. *E.S.* 18.6.1887, Standard Ironworks; 25.6.1887, 26.6.1897, Jubilee Celebrations; D.T-D. Clarke, *The Town Hall Colchester* (1972).
25. *E.S.* 4.9.1886, 7.5.1892, 9.7.1892, 4.2.1893, 8.7.1893, Town Council; 3.8.1894, Colchester.
26. *E.S.* 23.3.1895, 6.4.1895, 4.5.1895, 8.6.1895, 7.9.1895, 5.10.1895; *E.T.* 6.4.1895, Town Council; Correspondence, held by the Anglian Water Authority, between Davey Paxmans and the Waterworks Department.
27. *E.S.* 7.12.1895, 1.4.1896, Town Council; J.C. Thresh, *Essex Water Supply* (1901), p.137.
28. Calculations compiled from the Minutes of the Waterworks Committee and papers held by the Anglian Water Authority.

Chapter 10 Old Mortality
1. For example, Wood's 1890 Report p.3 gives a garrison population in 1889 of 3,886, the *Essex Standard* of 8.6.1889 a figure of 3,450, and the 1891 Census Returns 3,732.
2. For Colchester see Appendix A p.150; for England and Wales, calculated from Mitchell and Deane, *Abstract of British Historical Statistics* (1962), pp.36-37; for Leeds see B. Barber, 'Municipal Government in Leeds 1835-1914' in D. Fraser (ed.), *Municipal Reform and the Industrial City* (1982), p.67 and D. Fraser (ed.), *A History of Modern Leeds* (1980), p.64.
3. From figures printed in the *Essex Standard,* West Ham had a death rate of 30.2 for 1856-59. See also D.J. Olsen, *The Growth of Victorian London* (1979, Penguin Ed.), p.277.
4. A. Stewart and E. Jenkins, *Medical & Legal Aspects of Sanitary Reform 1867* (1969 Reprint), Table 4.
5. L.S. Col. Harvey Scrapbooks.
6. *E.S.* 5.12.1834, Colchester.
7. *E.S.* 11.1.1839, 10.1.1840, 14.1.1841, 4.2.1841, 18.2.1841, Relief of Poor; 22.1.1841, Letter; 13.1.1842, Labouring Classes. These public measures were also a comment on the shortcomings of the New Poor Law.
8. See Appendix A.
9. Ibid.; The saga of the High Street Market and its removal to Middleborough was a major Colchester controversy fought largely on economic rather than political lines. Newspaper references are too extensive to list, but see *E.S.* 9.2.1855, 31.5.1861. For Fred Philbrick's heroic stand see *E.S.* 27.2.1861, Town Council.
10. *E.S.* 29.2.1856, 4.9.1857, Colchester; 26.4.1861, 3.5.1871, 7.5.1881, 19.7.1891, *E.T.* 23.4.1901, Census Findings; Report of the Medical Officer of Health for 1901.
11. *E.S.* 11.11.1859, Registrar General; 10.2.1883, Town Council. There were also the inmates of the garrison hospital.
12. For Colchester see Appendix A; For England and Wales, Mitchell and Deane.
13. 1871 Census, Enumerators' Returns.
14. The attraction of London is noted by contemporaries and confirmed by Census returns: D. Friedlander and R. Roshier, 'A Study of Internal Migration in England & Wales' in *Population Studies* 19, March 1966; H. Le Caron, *Twenty-Five Years in the Secret Service* (1893), p.2. For most of the 19th century Colchester exported people. Only in the prosperous 1880s did the inter-censual population growth equal or exceed the surplus of births over deaths in the same decade.
15. M.W. Flinn, Introduction to Stewart & Jenkins, *Medical & Legal Aspects* (1969 Ed.)
16. *E.S.* 5.1.1884, Editorial.
17. *E.S.* 18.6.1887, Standard Iron Works Celebration; 14.6.1878, Land Sales; 7.9. 1878, 7.6.1879, 8.8.1885, Town Council; M.S.C. 1.1.1877, 18.4.1877, *E.T.* 3.3.1888, Leader.
18. *E.S.* 7.5.1873, Commissioners; See S.M. Gaskell, *Building Control; National Legislation and the Introduction of Local Byelaws in Victorian England* (1983). A copy of the 1877 Bye-Laws is in L.S. Col. 'Council Summonses etc.. 1862-96'
19. *E.T.* 6.10.1888, Town Council; Smith, *The People's Health,* p.103. Colchester's Dr Finch was dismissive of any connection between teething and diarrhoea, *E.S.* 10.9.1881, Town Council.
20. *E.T.* 6.10.1888, Town Council.
21. *E.S.* 6.2.1892, Town Council.
22. *E.S.* 17.11.1883, Letter; 10.9.1881, Town Council.
23. Smith, *The People's Health,* pp.85-100; Wohl, *Endangered Lives,* pp.20-36.
24. Calculated from Census Returns. The Colchester figures are considerably below the national rate which fell from 5.4 to 5.0 between 1851 and 1911. The distorting practice of calling tenement buildings a single 'house' partly explains the higher national rate. The figure for Lincoln, 4.75, was close to that of Colchester. See M.J. Daunton, 'Public Place & Private Space' in Fraser and Sutcliffe, *The Pursuit of Urban History,* p.253; Sir F. Hill, *Victorian Lincoln* (1974), p.156.
25. *E.S.* 10.11.1883, Guardians; 25.2.1874, Town Council.
26. Ibid.; *E.S.* 10.11.1883, Town Council.
27. *E.S.* 9.2.1884, Town Council.
28. For Colchester, Appendix A; For England and Wales, Mitchell & Deane.

29. *Essex Naturalist* Vol.16 (1911), pp.310-13.
30. See Appendix A.

Chapter 11 Requiescat
1. *E.S.* 25.6.1887, Jubilee Celebrations; 6.2.1892, Philbrick Obit; Hanham, *Elections & Party Management*, p.237.
2. E.T. 29.9.1883, Leader; 16.8.1890, Harvey Obit: *The Times* 13.3.1905, Harvey Obit.
3. *E.S.* 26.10.1889, Jones Obit; *E.T.* 26.10.1889, Jones Obit; *E.S.* 22.2.1890, Paxman Banquet.
4. *E.S.* 27.3.1874, Women's Suffrage; 10.12.1898, Hawkins Obit; Clarke, *Town Hall Colchester*, p.7.
5. *E.S.* 11.9.1886, Frinton; 11.6.1887, Colchester and County Notes; *E.A.D.T.* 26.2.1900, 2.3.1900, Bruff Obit; 24.5.1900, Bruff Auction; S.R.O. W39/3/1 Bruff's Will; Boyden, *Walton*, p.28. Of Bruff's five sons only one, Charles, remained close to him and attended the funeral. Charles Bruff played a characteristic role in the revival of the famous Coalport China Works, one of his father's more remarkable purchases. See Compton Mackenzie, *The House of Coalport 1750-1950* (1951).
6. *E.S.* 26. 6. 1886, Harwich Division; 22.3.1902, Suicide; 31.1.1905, Wicks Obit; *E.T.* 22.3.1902, Suicide; 31.1.1905, Wicks Obit.
7. For Marriage: *E.S.* 23.7.1932, Marriage Obit; R. Jenkins, *Asquith* (1964), p.542. For Paxman: *E.S.* 1.4.1922, Paxman Obit; Paxman Family Papers.
8. *E.S.* 16.9.1983, 23.9.1983, 30.12.1983, Jumbo; *Colchester Express* 30.9.1983.
9. *E.S.* 13.10.1978, 2.2.1979, 9.11.79, 16.4.1981, 14.7.1981, 13.8.1982, 20.8.1982, 23.9.1983, 30.9.1983, 23.3.1984 Culver Development.

INDEX

(Note: Unless otherwise stated, all streets, buildings and institutions listed are in Colchester)